THE TURBULENT 60s

1960

Other books in the
Turbulent 60s series:

1961
1962
1963
1964
1965
1966
1967
1968
1969

THE TURBULENT 60s

1960

Loreta M. Medina, *Book Editor*

Bonnie Szumski, *Publisher*
Scott Barbour, *Managing Editor*
David M. Haugen, *Series Editor*

**GREENHAVEN
PRESS** ®

THOMSON
TM
GALE

San Diego • Detroit • New York • San Francisco • Cleveland
New Haven, Conn. • Waterville, Maine • London • Munich

THOMSON
GALE

LIBRARY OF CONGRESS CATALOGING-IN-PUBLICATION DATA

1960 / Loreta M. Medina, book editor.
    p. cm. — (The turbulent 60s)
Includes bibliographical references and index.
ISBN 0-7377-1506-5 (alk. paper) — ISBN 0-7377-1507-3 (pbk. : alk. paper)
    1. United States—History—1953–1961—Sources. 2. Nineteen sixty, A.D.—Sources. I. Title: Nineteen sixty. II. Medina, Loreta M. III. Turbulent 60s
E835.A16 2004
973.921—dc22   2003049353

Printed in the United States of America

CONTENTS

Harvard University, brought his discovery of a psychedelic mushroom to Harvard and started the Center for Research in Personality, which studied the mushroom's uses in clinical psychology.

FOREWORD

The 1960s were a period of immense change in America. What many view as the complacency of the 1950s gave way to increased radicalism in the 1960s. The newfound activism of America's youth turned an entire generation against the social conventions of their parents. The rebellious spirit that marked young adulthood was no longer a stigma of the outcast but rather a badge of honor among those who wanted to remake the world. And in the 1960s, there was much to rebel against in America. The nation's involvement in Vietnam was one of the catalysts that helped galvanize young people in the early 1960s. Another factor was the day-to-day Cold War paranoia that seemed to be the unwelcome legacy of the last generation. And for black Americans in particular, there was the inertia of the civil rights movement that, despite seminal victories in the 1950s, had not effectively countered the racism still plaguing the country. All of these concerns prompted the young to speak out, to decry the state of the nation that would be their inheritance.

The 1960s, then, may best be remembered for its spirit of confrontation. The student movement questioned American imperialism, militant civil rights activists confronted their elders over the slow progress of change, and the flower children faced the nation's capitalistic greed and conservative ethics and opted to create a counterculture. There was a sense of immediacy to all this activism, and people put their bodies on the line to bring about change. Although there were reactionaries and conservative holdouts, the general feeling was that a united spirit of resistance could stop the inevitability of history. People could shape their own destinies, and together they could make a better world. As sixties chronicler Todd Gitlin writes, "In the Sixties it seemed especially true that History with a capital H had come down to earth, either interfering with life or making it possible: and that within History, or threaded through it, people were living with a supercharged density: lives were bound up with one another, making claims on one another, drawing one another into the common project."

Perhaps not everyone experienced what Gitlin describes, but few would argue that the nation as a whole was left untouched by the radical notions of the times. The women's movement, the civil rights movement, and the antiwar movement left indelible marks. Even the hippie movement left behind a relaxed morality and a more ecological mindset. Popular culture, in turn, reflected these changes: Music became more diverse and experimental, movies adopted more adult themes, and fashion attempted to replicate the spirit of uninhibited youth. It seemed that every facet of American culture was affected by the pervasiveness of revolution in the 1960s, and despite the diversity of rebellions, there remained a sense that all were related to, as Gitlin puts it, "the common project."

Of course, this communal zeitgeist of the 1960s is best attributed to the decade in retrospect. The 1960s were not a singular phenomenon but a progress of individual days, of individual years. Greenhaven Press follows this rubric in The Turbulent Sixties series. Each volume of this series is devoted to the major events that define a specific year of the decade. The events are discussed in carefully chosen articles. Some of these articles are written by historians who have the benefit of hindsight, but most are contemporary accounts that reveal the complexity, confusion, excitement, and turbulence of the times. Each article is prefaced by an introduction that places the event in its historical context. Every anthology is also introduced by an essay that gives shape to the entire year. In addition, the volumes in the series contain time lines, each of which gives an at-a-glance structure to the major events of the topic year. A bibliography of helpful sources is also provided in each anthology to offer avenues for further study. With these tools, readers will better understand the developments in the political arena, the civil rights movement, the counterculture, and other facets of American society in each year. And by following the trends and events that define the individual years, readers will appreciate the revolutionary currents of this tumultuous decade—the turbulent sixties.

The Year of Agitation

I n 1960 the Cold War dynamic between the United States and the Soviet Union dominated the national scene, and the mood it created was that of agitation. Subduing Soviet threats preoccupied Dwight D. Eisenhower's presidency and defined his administration's domestic and foreign policy. The same threats infringed on the lives of ordinary Americans. Regular warnings of possible nuclear attacks were issued, and people were encouraged to build bomb shelters in their homes.

Of the belligerent nature of the superpower rivalry, authors Laurence Chang and Peter Kornbluh observe the following: "U.S.-Soviet relations were characterized by recurring conflict. Many issues, including the accelerating nuclear arms race, U.S. deployment of weapons along the Soviet periphery, Soviet support for revolutions in the Third World, and most important, the unresolved status of Berlin, inflamed superpower tensions and sustained fears on both sides that the Cold War might escalate into some form of open military conflict."[1]

Throughout the year there was a deeply felt sense that the United States was in a permanent state of war with its ideological enemy. There was an unprecedented rush in the country's buildup of war weapons, including nuclear-tipped missiles that could strike Russia in minutes. Sometime during the year, the U.S. military launched the nation's most modern, sophisticated, and destructive weapon—the nuclear-armed *George Washington* submarine whose destructive capacity equaled "all the explosives used . . . in World War II."[2] Deployed in the North Atlantic, the submarine was meant to deliver the message to the Soviet Union that the United States could retaliate against nuclear attack from anywhere in the world. Also inaugurated in the same year was a $500 million radar system that could detect Soviet missile launches seconds after launch and activate the country's defense network to respond in minutes.

Behind the frenzied production of weapons was the constant threat of the so-called "missile gap." The U.S. government feared that Russia had in its arsenal more medium-range and long-range missiles than America had. Soviet premier Nikita Khrushchev continued to boast that Russia had more intercontinental ballistic missiles (ICBMs) than the United States and that it could deliver a devastating attack on American soil any time. The missile gap was finally resolved in mid-1961 when U.S. intelligence concluded the missile gap favored the United States. According to Chang and Kornbluh, the United States had 170 long-range missiles, compared to the Soviet Union's 20 to 40; it also had 3,000 nuclear warheads, compared to the Soviet's 250.

Eisenhower's Challenges

Before 1961, however, the only way the United States could confirm Soviet claims of arms supremacy was to fly planes that would take photographs of suspected missile sites. On May 1, 1960, President Eisenhower approved one such reconnaissance operation. Tensions rose dangerously when Khrushchev announced that his military had shot down the U.S. plane and had captured its pilot. The Soviet leader loudly protested the act and warned of serious repercussions if the United States continued its espionage activities.

Many Americans were disappointed that Eisenhower had initially denied his knowledge about the spy plane, but he refused to apologize to the Soviets for the incursion. On the global level, the May Day incident dashed all hopes of further discussions on disarmament and the ban on further nuclear testing. But this was not the only test of America's Cold War resolve. In Asia, communism was gaining inroads in Laos and Vietnam, and just a few miles from the U.S. southern border, Fidel Castro had just ended the rule of Fulgencio Batista and was steering Cuba toward the Soviet orbit. Not wishing to turn the Cold War hot, Eisenhower found it nearly impossible to contain the spread of communism and Soviet influence. The popularity of his administration suffered for its perceived "soft" stance on Soviet strategems.

At year's end, Eisenhower's presidency culminated. A general with a stellar record during World War II, he warned of the dangerous repercussions of a relentless arms buildup. Throughout his term, he had restrained powerful industrial lobbies that advocated a stockpiling of supplies and weapons. Just before leaving office, he pointed to a huge "military-industrial complex" that had ominous influence on national security and could, if unchecked, create a "militarized America."[3]

Mass Action Against Segregation

While most Americans were absorbed with the Cold War, black communities in the South were on their way to waging another kind of war. A nascent student movement was beginning to stir, setting its sights on ending segregation, alleviating the plight of black Americans, and bringing about meaningful social reform.

In 1960 black students decided they could no longer be silent and started defying legally sanctioned segregation by asserting their presence in facilities traditionally designated as "for whites only," including buses, restaurants, libraries, galleries, beaches, and others. It was the year when black communities joined forces to protest their marginalization by white American society.

Historian Arthur Marwick, writing in *The Sixties: The Cultural Revolution in Britain, France, Italy, and the United States*, singles out the importance of the 1960 black student protests and their impact. He says: "When we think of the sixties we think of student protests, and the students we usually have in mind are French students on the Paris barricades in 1968, or perhaps white American students at Berkeley in 1964. Yet, historically, the most important single set of student protests was that of the southern black colleges in 1960."[4]

To a large extent, the year would be remembered as the time when the civil rights movement, steered by youngsters, proved that the march of blacks toward integration and social change could no longer be stopped. Author and historian Terry H. Anderson, writing in *The Movement and the Sixties: Protest in America from Greensboro to Wounded Knee*, claims the student protests in 1960 "launched the 1960s."[5]

A Quiet Start

On February 1, 1960, four black first-year students at North Carolina Agricultural and Technical College (NCAT) sat down at the lunch counter of the local Woolworth store in Greensboro and asked to be served at an area traditionally reserved for whites. The waitress adamantly refused to serve them, but the young men remained steadfast. The students continued to sit at the counter, registering their protest for the rest of the afternoon. The young protesters later confessed they had launched their daunting act because they were tired of being discriminated against in public facilities, were impatient with the acquiescence of their elders, and were desperate to do their share in putting an end to segregation.

Little did the young men know that their small, seemingly isolated act on that February morning would trigger more lunch-counter protests in other black communities. Their nonviolent defiance reverberated across southern states and would touch not only students, but also older civil rights workers, church leaders, seasoned activists, white sympathizers, and some sections of the general public.

After reading about the North Carolina student protesters in a newspaper, Robert Moses, a young black man from New York, expressed his awe: "Before, the Negro in the South had always looked on the defensive, cringing. This time they were taking the initiative. They were kids my age, and I knew this had something to do with my own life. It made me realize that for a long time I had been troubled by the problem of being a Negro and at the same time being an American. This was the answer."[6]

News about the Greensboro incident spread throughout the South like wildfire. Soon blacks would use colleges and churches as places for recruitment, planning, and organization. They would launch sit-down protests at lunch counters in Winston-Salem, Durham, Raleigh, and other cities across North Carolina. Historian Terry H. Anderson notes that by the end of February activists were using the tactic employed in Greensboro in seven states and more than thirty communities including Nashville, Tallahassee, Chattanooga, Richmond, and Baltimore. In the following months students were flooding white-only facilities in Charleston, Columbia, Miami, Houston, San Antonio, and Xenia (Ohio).

Local and Regional Organization

The protests would eventually lead to the formation in April 1960 of the Student Nonviolent Coordinating Committee (SNCC), which aimed to develop autonomous local movements for desegregation, using nonviolent means. This mandate of self-direction would, in later years, set the student organization on a collision course with the older civil rights groups such as the National Association for the Advancement of Colored People (NAACP), the Congress of Racial Equality (CORE), the Urban League, and the

Southern Christian Leadership Conference (SCLC). To the members of SNCC (pronounced "snick"), these other groups—typically made up of older activists—were not pressing hard enough for immediate change. Of the pivotal role that SNCC consequently played in igniting mass protests in the South and elsewhere, history professor Clayborne Carson, a key participant in the civil rights movement, declares:

> SNCC's founding was an important step on the transformation of a limited student movement to desegregate lunch counters into a broad and sustained movement to achieve major social reforms. . . . The existence of a South-wide coordinating committee provided the opportunity for increasing numbers of young people to participate in a regional movement that would attack racism in all its dimensions.[7]

SNCC chose to work with local communities as a strategy in developing organizations at the local level. From community to community, students exchanged information on their experiences and trained new participants in nonviolent methods. Throughout 1960 the students initiated and organized hundreds of protest actions across the South, thrusting the issues of segregation, inequality, and injustice in the face of the whole nation. The picket line was no longer limited to a store's lunch counter; it had expanded to include a large section of the country.

Demonstrations continued throughout 1961, and by the end of that year the students had achieved extraordinary successes. In about two hundred other cities, including Greensboro, Houston, and Atlanta, lunch counters and theaters had integrated. In two years young students had started a social movement that had already dismantled the traditional social barriers in the South.

Continuation of Desegregation

The lunch-counter sit-ins continued the work of the civil rights movement, which has its roots in the 1954 U.S. Supreme Court ruling that declared segregated schools unconstitutional. The sit-down protests were reminiscent of several challenges blacks had waged against segregation in the 1950s, the most prominent of which was the yearlong bus boycott in Montgomery, Alabama, in December 1955. The boycott protested the imprisonment of Rosa Parks, a member of the local community, after she refused to give her bus seat to a white person.

The memory of Montgomery, made sharp by the moral fervor and charisma of its key leader Reverend Martin Luther King Jr., may have been in the minds of the Greensboro students and the rest of the protesters in the South. The protests' showcase of local action must have provided the Greensboro students an important lesson in communities working together. However, the Greensboro protests were one step ahead of the Montgomery boycott: They triggered sustained actions in the South. Of this new dimension in black political advancement, author and historian Terry H. Anderson comments: "The lunch-counter sit-ins . . . were a decisive break with earlier civil rights demonstrations and with cold war culture. The sit-ins ignited a young generation of blacks to become activists, and more important, they stimulated some southern and many northern whites to participate in something they began calling 'the movement.'"[8]

Race Becomes a National Issue

The early protests in 1960 would eventually move whites in the North, who had historically held the South in contempt, and lead the former to take action. The SNCC students provided a link to white students in the North who, in Arthur Marwick's words, "felt the call to play their part in the fight against segregation."[9] White students from northern colleges began actively participating in the May 1961 freedom rides, which aimed to demolish segregation in bus stations.

The brutality and violence that met the freedom rides and subsequent mass protests—brought home by television—indelibly marked the imagery of the civil rights movement in the South in the early sixties. The visibility of race relations could no longer be ignored by those in power. An issue initially believed to be specific to the South could no longer be contained only in the South—it had become a national issue.

Arthur Marwick cites the most important success of the student protests as "the achievement of universal visibility on the part of those determined to reveal and contest the injustices suffered by blacks, and the revelation that these injustices were so deeply imbricated in so many different aspects of American society that trying to overcome them was going to involve violence, destruction, and . . . positive action."[10]

The impulse that revved up student protests in the South would surface in other places. In Southern California, where the case of Caryl Chessman had been playing out for several years, thousands upon thousands of sympathizers staged protests to voice their indignation over the death penalty. Chessman, convicted in 1948 of several felony counts, was going to die in the gas chamber as mandated by California law.

Chessman's case not only generated local protests that involved all strata of society, but it created an international controversy. Thousands of petitions coming as far as Brazil, Switzerland, the Vatican, and others poured into the judicial system. Chessman was finally put to death on May 2, 1960, but his case would have long-term repercussions. It would influence the debate on capital punishment in later years.

In another scene, the House Un-American Activities Committee (HUAC), a government watchdog against communism, continued its much-feared surveillance of persons it suspected of being Communists or supporting communism. In May 1960, eight thousand students from the University of California at Berkeley and other Bay Area colleges, joined by artists and rebels, demonstrated at San Francisco City Hall to protest HUAC's activities. The May 1960 student protests, directed against HUAC's incursions on civil liberties, might have been limited, but they clearly set into motion an unstoppable force—student militancy in the sixties.

The stirrings of agitation first felt in the South in 1960 would rise to a pitch in the coming years as students became a bulwark of protest and dissent. Whether from the North or South, rich or poor, in colleges or in streets, they took to the streets in massive numbers, challenging institutions, espousing new values, championing new liberties, urging for peace, and eventually transforming the United States in ways few Americans had earlier imagined.

Notes

1. Laurence Chang and Peter Kornbluh, *The Cuban Missile Crisis, 1962: A National Security Archive Documents Reader.* New York: New Press, 1998, p. 1.

2. Stephen King-Hall, "Cold War Under the Sea," *Nation,* December 27, 1960, p. 495.

3. Elmo Richardson, *The Presidency of Dwight D. Eisenhower.* Lawrence: Regents Press of Kansas, 1979, p. 185.

4. Arthur Marwick, *The Sixties: Cultural Revolution in Britain, France,*

Italy, and the United States. Oxford: Oxford University Press, 1998, p. 204.

5. Terry H. Anderson, *The Movement and the Sixties: Protest in America from Greensboro to Wounded Knee.* New York: Oxford University Press, 1995, p. 47.

6. Quoted in Clayborne Carson, *In Struggle: SNCC and the Black Awakening of the 1960s.* Cambridge: Harvard University Press, 1981, p. 17.

7. Carson, *In Struggle*, p. 19.

8. Anderson, *The Movement and the Sixties*, p. 45.

9. Marwick, *The Sixties*, p. 204.

10. Marwick, *The Sixties*, p. 207.

Greensboro Sit-in Sparks Action Against Segregation

By Jim Schlosser

In the following 1998 article, the four black students speak about the day they sat at the lunch counter, strictly reserved for whites, of the local Woolworth store in Greensboro, North Carolina. Three of the four young men—Franklin McCain, Joseph McNeil, and Ezell Blair Jr.—recall the moments when they were planning the protest action as well as the time they were actually sitting at the counter, firm but also fearful that they would be beaten up and jailed. The four started the protest out of their conviction that segregation was wrong. They also acted out of disappointment over their elders' indifference in the past. Author Jim Schlosser calls the four young students heroes, arguing that they quickened the pace of the civil rights movement and hastened integration in the South. Schlosser asserts that in their act of sitting at the counter, the young men were attacking the social order of the time. Jim Schlosser is a staff writer at the *News & Record* in Greensboro.

I t's more amusing than ironic what's happening now, 38 years later. Everybody wants to be part of a winner, even those who weren't cheering for victory in the beginning.

On Feb. 1, 1960, the Greensboro Four, as they would later be called, felt isolated and alone as they sat at that whites-only lunch counter at the Woolworth Store on South Elm Street.

They were seeking more than what they ordered—sodas, coffee, doughnuts. They were attacking the social order of the time. The unwritten rules of society required black people to stay out of white-owned restaurants, to use only designated drinking fountains and restrooms, to sit in the rear of Greensboro city buses, in a separate balcony at the Center Theatre and in segregated bleachers during sports events at War Memorial Stadium.

The Four Students

The four black youths—Franklin McCain, Joseph McNeil, Ezell Blair Jr. and David Richmond, all still teenagers and all freshmen on academic scholarships at N.C. A&T State University—had entered the unknown. McCain, who grew up in Washington and spent one year attending Greensboro's Dudley High School, says he expected to be arrested, beaten to a pulp or worse.

All four would emerge unscathed and eventually be recognized as heroes of the civil rights movement.

They were persistent. In the days after Feb. 1, they would be joined by other students at the Woolworth counter and at the Kress 5 & 10 lunch counter a half-block away. Their protests inspired black people to do the same at Formica-topped dime-store counters in other cities. The movement they started led to the integration of the Woolworth and the Kress chains, landmarks on every main street in the South.

Today [in 1998], the three surviving members of the Greensboro Four laugh and make room for all who claim they were with them in person or in spirit 38 years ago at the counter.

Franklin McCain concedes he can't remember everybody, of course, because by the fourth and fifth day of the sit-ins, the original four had grown to hundreds of demonstrators downtown. But many of the participants lacked the patience to sit for long periods of time while spectators heckled and stared at them.

"What people won't talk (about), what people don't like to remember is that the success of that movement in Greensboro is probably attributed to no more than eight or 10 people," McCain says. "I can say this: when the television cameras stopped rolling and we didn't have eight or 10 reporters left, the folks left. I mean, there were just a very faithful few. McNeil and I can't count the nights and evenings that we literally cried because we couldn't get people to help us staff a picket line."

The three surviving members of the Greensboro Four—David

Richmond of Greensboro died in 1990, 11 months after a huge 30th anniversary commemoration of the sit-ins—recently recalled their feelings on that Feb. 1 and what led them to make such a bold move. They discussed who, if anyone, knew of their plans in advance. They talked about, and dismissed, claims made in recent years that they were serving as substitutes for Bennett College female students.

The three men talked about the unlikely supporters they encountered—from the elderly white woman who cheered them on that first day to the city's richest man at the time, Spencer Love, who was determined that no blood would be spilt in his city.

They also talked about why they dared take on a system so deeply ingrained in the city and South.

"From my perspective, it was a down payment on manhood," McNeil said. "The secret of life is known when to take on something difficult and to take something on that might have enormous risks and implications."

The Greensboro Four acted at a time when protests against segregation in schools and on buses were taking place in the South, led by the Rev. Martin Luther King Jr. But there were few challenges to segregation in privately owned businesses, such as Woolworth. The thinking was that a man's business was an extension of his home. It was his castle, and he had the right of association.

In this case, the man with the keys to the castle was Clarence "Curly" Harris, the long-time manager of the Woolworth store on South Elm Street, one of the most prosperous in the Woolworth chain. Harris had been reading in the newspapers about growing black resistance in the South. In a rare interview, the 92-year-old Harris says he sensed the four teenagers at his lunch counter would not go away easily.

He recalls calling his supervisor, who told him not to worry, that the students would give up soon and the incident would blow over without harm to the store's robust sales. Harris disagreed.

The sit-ins lasted off and on for five months before Woolworth and the Kress store down the street agreed to integrate.

Memories of a Different Time

Today, millions visit the Smithsonian Institution and see the photos that Jack Moebes, a *Greensboro News & Record* photographer at the time, took on the first and second days of the sit-ins.

Four stools and a section of the counter from the store are also part of the display.

Until the store closed in 1995, a sit-in commemoration was held there every five years on Feb. 1. The Greensboro Four would return. Woolworth always sent a vice president from its New York headquarters to tell how the company now embraced diversity. City of Greensboro officials, so nervous during the sit-ins, would be there beaming.

Memories are dimming about the way things used to be in Greensboro and the South. Men and women under the age of 40 have no memory of the sit-ins, or of the strict segregation that defined every aspect of life.

Today, young people looked astonished when told that at the old city hall on Greene Street, two side-by-side water fountains stood in the corridor—one for whites, the other for blacks.

Some black parents kept their children from going downtown and being exposed to such a degrading social system. Others, like Ezell Blair Jr., who now goes by the name Jibreel Khazan, showed at an early age that he wasn't afraid to go against the social order.

Getting Tired of Segregation

Segregation's pervasiveness was such that black people couldn't escape it. Joseph McNeil got off a bus at Union Station downtown in January 1960, returning from a visit to his home in Wilmington over the Christmas vacation. He was hungry. The station had a restaurant. He wasn't allowed to sit down and eat.

His outrage accompanied him back to Scott Hall, where that night he and his roommate, Greensboro native David Richmond, gathered with McCain and another Greensboro native, Blair, both of whom bunked down the hall. Since entering school the previous autumn, they had held on-going gripe sessions in their Scott Hall rooms about life in the South.

"I was getting tired of just talking about it," McCain says, "and McNeil said he was, too."

Many times they had attacked previous generations of black people, including their own parents and university administrators, for what the four perceived as a weak response to segregation. McCain told his friends by just talking and doing nothing, they were no better.

Potential targets for protest were plentiful, from the city buses, where black people had to ride in the rear, to the county jail, where separate cells were reserved for black inmates.

The four freshmen selected Woolworth. They especially resented the company's double standard. Everywhere but in the South, black and white patrons sat together at Woolworth counters. In Greensboro, not only was the counter segregated, but so was the staff behind it and in the kitchen upstairs. Waitresses were white; those who fixed the food and cleaned up were black.

Black patrons could shop Woolworth's general merchandise counters and eat at a stand-up snack bar and bakery counter. But one section of the store was forbidden territory: the long L-shaped lunch counter, with stainless steel and plastic cushion stools that took up nearly two walls of the first floor.

Until 1958, Woolworth posted "colored only" and "whites only" signs in the store to guide the two races. That year, Dr. George Simkins, who had led fights in the city to desegregate municipal-owned facilities, such as tennis courts and libraries, asked Harris to remove the signs. Harris agreed to do so, but only if another downtown store did the same. Simkins said Belk Department Store up the street had made such a commitment. Harris wasn't worried about the effects of removing the signs. He knew black customers didn't need signs to know what was off limits.

The assumption in Greensboro always has been that nothing happens on the civil rights front without Simkins, local National Association for the Advancement of Colored People (NAACP) president from 1959 to 1984, knowing about it beforehand. He was a major risk-taker, having gone to jail in 1955 for trespassing at city-owned Gillespie Park Golf Course, where he and a group of black friends attempted to play a round. The governor later pardoned him.

But Simkins says the sit-ins surprised him. He had been at his office filling cavities when a reporter first called to inform him that something was happening at the Woolworth store downtown.

McCain and McNeil say no one outside the group knew of their plans, although Khazan insists that the four went to his parents' house in Greensboro the night before to tell his parents.

The three also say they didn't discuss in advance their plans with Ralph Johns, a white merchant who had long been exhorting black customers at his store on East Market Street to challenge the city's racist ways. He promised bail money to anyone who was arrested in the cause of freedom. . . .

On That Fateful Day

The fact that the four students were acting alone made the hours leading up to Feb. 1 more miserable. They say they barely slept the night before the sit-ins started. Then they had a full day of classes on Monday. It was after 3 P.M. before Richmond, Blair and McNeil made it to the designated spot, outside Bluford Library, where they waited for McCain, who had a late Air Force ROTC class.

They walked up East Market Street, through the railroad underpass that still serves as the dividing point between the black and white communities of Greensboro. McCain wore his Air Force uniform. He says many people later asked him if this was his way of protesting the Vietnam War. Never mind, he says laughing, that serious American involvement in Vietnam hadn't even started in 1960. Others were sure the uniform was a patriotic symbol and a tactic: How could a business deny service to a young man wearing the uniform of his country? That wasn't the reason for uniform either, he says. He says he just didn't have time to go back to his room and change.

The four passed Ralph Johns' store and hinted to him that they were up to something. Johns must have figured out what was happening. He went into the store and called Jo Spivey, a reporter for *The Greensboro Record*, the afternoon paper.

As the four turned onto South Elm Street at Jefferson Square, McCain had awful thoughts about what might happen to him in the store whose familiar red sign was looming ahead.

"I can tell you this," he said. "I was fully prepared mentally not to ever come back to the campus. . . . I thought the worst thing that could happen to us is we could have had our heads split open with a night stick and hauled into prison."

At Woolworth, the four split up in pairs and went to various counters to buy toothpaste and school supplies. The strategy was to ask why they could be served in other parts of the store, but not at the lunch counter. McNeil and McCain were the first to take seats at the counter, where about 12 white people were taking afternoon coffee breaks.

They had expected a ruckus. They encountered silence. It was as if they were invisible. Waitresses ignored them.

Geneva Tisdale, a black employee who was working behind the counter, figured the four young men were confused out-of-towners who didn't know the ways of Greensboro.

"I just thought there was somebody here from someplace else that didn't know they didn't serve blacks," she said, "so I kept on doing what I was doing."

She changed her mind when the four finally got the attention of a waitress, who told them black people weren't served at the counter. When they refused to leave, a black employee—not Tisdale—gave the students a lecture on how they were troublemakers hurting race relations.

Curly Harris was next to talk to the students.

When the four men wouldn't budge from their seats, Harris hurried to the police station two blocks away to see Chief Paul Calhoun. The unflappable chief said that as long as the students behaved, he could do nothing. He did dispatch a police officer to keep an eye on the store.

An Exhilarating Experience

Then came a sign from heaven, McCain is convinced. An elderly white woman came up to them.

"She said, 'Boys, I am just so proud of you. My only regret is that you didn't do this 10 or 15 years ago,'" McCain recalls. "Well, 10 or 15 years ago, my goodness, I was only 8 or 10 years old, but I got the message and I can tell you that that simple acknowledgment and pat on the shoulder meant more to me that day than anything else. . . . I got so much pride and such a good

Four black students stage a sit-in at the lunch counter of a Woolworth store in Greensboro, North Carolina.

positive feeling from that little old lady. I mean, she'll never know it, but that really made the day for us."

Back from the police station, Harris announced the store was closing early. The four students filed out, unserved but not deterred. They told Harris they would be back the next day.

Outside, on Sycamore Street, the four encountered *Record* photographer Jack Moebes, who carried a big, boxy Speed Graphic camera that even by 1960 was outdated. Moebes got a picture of the students walking four abreast from the store.

On the walk back to campus, McCain said he felt like he was floating.

"I've never felt so good in my life," he said. "I truly felt as though I had my going-to-the-mountaintop experience."

Back on campus that night, they rounded up leaders of student groups and held a meeting in the basement of Dudley Building. The four sought pledges of help the next day. Instead, they had to explain themselves. No one believed what they had done.

The four finally managed to convince the majority present that this was no joke. Many in the room pledged to join them the next day.

All of two people showed up to join the original four at the store. They sat from 11 A.M. to 3 P.M. They were not served. Several white people heckled them. But again, they left unharmed and without being arrested. Channel 2 sent a cameraman. *The Daily News* and *The Record* had reporters present. Once the news hit the TV, radio and the newspapers, Agriculture and Technology (A&T) students embraced the movement. Each day after that, more and more joined the original four. By that Saturday, students from A&T and Bennett, joined by sympathetic white students from UNCG, Greensboro College, and Guilford College, occupied every seat at the counter.

Curly Harris was outraged. He could see sales figures plummeting.

Geneva Tisdale was scared. Some rough-looking white people had started coming to the store to heckle the protesters. She heard some were Ku Klux Klan members. She was expecting a baby and was fearful of what stress might do to her pregnancy. The lunch counter manager, Rachel Holt, sent Tisdale upstairs to the kitchen so she wouldn't be exposed to ugliness. Finally, with the counter virtually shut down because of the sit-ins, Tisdale's boss sent her home.

In addition to occupying seats inside, students formed picket lines along South Elm and Sycamore streets to discourage people from shopping at Woolworth and Kress. . . .

The city created a committee, headed by Burlington Industries executive Ed Zane, to mediate the stand-off and to discuss segregation in the downtown. The Greensboro Four would say later that Zane turned out to be a hero, along with his boss, Spencer Love, the founder of Burlington Industries. Love was determined that the violence he saw in other Southern cities wasn't going to happen in Greensboro.

Initial Success

Finally, Woolworth and Kress agreed to integrate. It was a humanitarian and a business decision, Curly Harris says.

The Greensboro Four wouldn't have the honor of eating the first meal at the integrated counter. Geneva Tisdale and two other black kitchen workers at Woolworth were the first. Holt, the counter manager, told them to wear their Sunday best. Tisdale remembers ordering an egg salad sandwich and a soda. The egg salad was good because she had made it herself earlier that morning. She regrets there were no cameras in the store to record the history.

"They never knew that it was Woolworth girls that was the first to sit at the counter to be served after they opened it up," she said.

The Greensboro Four returned to their studies. All but Richmond went on to earn degrees. The three survivors are called on constantly for interviews that turn up in articles and books and documentaries. They say they never expected to become celebrities and that it has its drawbacks. People constantly ask McCain what have you done for the human race lately.

McCain says he feels better about America today than he did in 1960. He says he loves his country so much that he wants to kiss the ground after he returns from business trips abroad. McNeil says he believes in the fundamental goodness of people, white and black.

He fought for civil rights in the 1960s and then fought again as an Air Force officer during the Vietnam War later in the decade.

"This is my country," he says. "I not only fought for it, I fought for the chance to make it right. No one's going to deny me the opportunity. I am going to be a full participant in every aspect of this community, as well as my kids."

Our Compact Cars: The Score to Date

By James C. Jones and John A. Conway

In this February 8, 1960, article, James C. Jones and John A. Conway
see the frenzied manufacture of compact cars at the start of 1960 as a
revolution. For first-quarter production alone, set at 2.3 million units—
the highest in history—compacts will comprise 20 to 25 percent. The
authors cite industry experts who predict that 7 million cars will be
sold in 1960, and 1.7 million of them will be compacts. Competing for
a share in this huge market are the Big Three—General Motors, Ford,
and Chrysler—racing against American Motors, Studebaker-Packard,
and their foreign rivals. An industry leader predicts that by 1963, half
of U.S. cars sold will be compacts.

Jones and Conway note that some quarters of the car business are
concerned that compact cars will reduce sales of medium-priced cars
and used cars. Foreign car manufacturers, however, view the trend pos-
itively. With a 10 percent-share in U.S. sales, they believe that small
cars will widen the appeal of foreign cars. At the time of writing, Jones
was *Newsweek*'s Detroit bureau chief and Conway, an associate editor.

T he nation's auto dealers converged on Washington this
week to trade shoptalk, fret about profit margins, and discuss what was new and interesting—and the newest and
most interesting thing on the scene was a perky, 195-inch rascal
that paraded under the name of Comet. It was Ford Motor Co.'s

second compact car (to be handled by Mercury dealers), latest U.S. entry in the compact-car race.

Latest, but by no means the last. Before the year is out, auto buyers will be lining up to see four more compacts. General Motors will bring out three, one each for Buick, Oldsmobile, and Pontiac dealers. Chrysler will have a compact for its Dodge salesmen. Added to the already introduced Falcon, Corvair, and Valiant, that will mean eight new auto name plates in the space of twelve months. Detroit hasn't had that many christenings a year in 30 years.[1]

It all adds up to a revolution in the auto business. And the most surprising thing about the whole trend is that automakers say they still aren't sure how big a market there is for the compacts. "Come back in 90 days," says Chrysler vice president Byron Nichols.

But if they aren't certain, they must have some pretty solid hunches. Otherwise, the decisions they're making would amount to simple foolhardiness.

First-quarter production schedules have been stepped up to the highest level in history—almost 2.3 million units. Some 20-to-25 per cent of that output probably will be compacts, and to turn out that share the industry is shifting its production facilities like so many pieces on a giant checkerboard. Ford general manager James Wright, for instance, now aims to turn out up to 500,000 Falcons in 1960 vs. an original target of 300,000. He has had to put the Falcon on truck-assembly lines in Kansas City and California in addition to Falcon's original plant in Lorain, Ohio. To get his 9,000 Corvairs a week, Chevrolet general manager E.N. Cole had to evict trucks from the Willow Run plant in Michigan, and squeeze more of his rear-engine autos onto truck lines at two other sites. Chrysler started out to make 4,400 Valiants a week in its huge Dodge main plant in Hamtramck, Mich., pressed St. Louis into service for another 1,600, and this month will start making still another 1,500 weekly in Delaware.

Nor are American Motors and Studebaker-Packard standing still. American Motors president George Romney, now shooting at a 1960 sales target of 500,000 Ramblers, is spending $51 mil-

---

1. Of the four still-to-come compacts, Pontiac's is the only one which has yet been named. Tentatively, it's to be called Vanguard. Ford will also bring out a compact truck, called the Ranchito, this month. And, in case the demand ever develops, it has in the works a definitely small car in the Volkswagen class, which will probably weigh about 1,500 pounds (vs. 2,366 pounds for the Falcon) and have a 95-inch wheel base (vs. 109½ inches).

lion to step up eventual capacity of 700,000 cars a year. The Lark, Studebaker's lifesaving little wonder, has added a new touch—the first compact convertible.

Sales for the first twenty days of January gave automen more than a bit of encouragement as they stepped up production schedules. During the first weeks of the year, U.S. plants sold 282,000 new cars, and the experts over at *Ward's Automotive Reports* now expect the month's total to hit 460,000 (including about 115,000 compacts). Adding in 50,000 imports means a grand total of 510,000 sales, a scant 2,000 below the all-time record of January 1955. Some Detroiters, in fact, expect to see the old mark topped. And most of them hold to a prediction of 7 million cars sold—1.7 million of them compacts—in 1960.

Automen are still collecting and analyzing late sales returns to find out how the different compacts are doing. Back in November, Rambler accounted for 22 per cent of all compact and economy car sales. Falcon had 20 per cent, Corvair 10, Lark 8, Valiant 3, and all imports 37.

But November was not a normal month. Most people were just getting their first real look at the cars. Steel shortages crippled production of Corvairs and Valiants. So the compact car standings probably will change. And, in fact, the industry estimates that Falcon inched ahead of Rambler in the first twenty days of January.

Testimonials

If they needed any testimonials for the pulling power of the compacts, automakers had only to turn to the perennially optimistic auto dealers. A St. Louis Plymouth dealer went so far as to hail the Valiant as "the salvation of the automobile business." New York's Don Allen agency, which handles Corvairs, reports: "We haven't seen activity like this since right after the war." "We have not had enough cars in stock to do the job we could do," says a Falcon dealer on Van Ness Avenue, San Francisco's automobile row.

While they may not yet know the exact number of potential compact-car customers, automakers are getting a better idea of what the customers—be they 1 million or 2 million—are like—and what they want. One clue: American motorists appear to want more horsepower than the compacts originally offered. Result: Valiant offers an optional power kit which boosts its engine rating from 101 hp to 148; Falcon, with a standard 90-hp engine, has joined the parade with an optional 128-hp engine. Corvair, too, has an optional engine—of 95-hp, 15 horsepower more than its standard powerplant. Insurance companies, which grant discounts on premiums for compact cars, haven't reacted officially to this small-scale horsepower race. For insurance purposes, they have set a 125-hp limit on compact cars.

Should the new compact cars prove out their promise of a whopping success, the impact, of course, will spread across the auto industry. Detroit's biggest problem: Sales of compact cars may be at the expense of its standard models.

So far, automakers insist that this hasn't and won't happen. "We forecast enough expansion in the new-car market—15 to 20 per cent—so that it would absorb the compacts without detracting from the standard lines," says Chevrolet's Cole. Ford's Wright figures that 34 per cent of the Falcon buyers were added starters to the new-car market. (Coincidentally, a Chevrolet survey in Pittsburgh yielded exactly the same figure—34 per cent of Corvair sales were "clean deals," that is, the purchases were made without a trade-in.)

Nevertheless, there is at least one unsettling sign that sales of standard cars may suffer from the insurgent compacts. Auto sales this year have been running about 8 per cent ahead of 1959—17,643 a day vs. 16,320—but sales of the full-grown Ford lag 800 units a day behind the year-ago pace.

Medium-priced cars may also feel the competitive pinch. Ford's Comet is the first "luxury" compact. The remaining four compacts scheduled for introduction this year are also designed for the same market. So medium-priced dealers will be competing against themselves with the new models, all the while fighting off the sallies of the low-priced autos which nibble away at their bigger brothers' markets with luxury models of their own.

All this could have a heavy impact on automakers' revenues. Ford's two-door Falcon, for instance, carries a factory wholesale tag of $1,525 vs. $1,704 for the two-door Fairlane. The company must thus sell 111 or 112 Falcons to match the gross of 100 Fairlanes. For the auto dealer, so far, the ratio is better—40 two-door Falcons equal the gross of 39 two-door Fairlanes. But this will change when discounting, now only an isolated phenomenon, becomes more widespread on the new small cars.

The customers, however, are giving the industry a lift by eagerly ordering all the accessories in sight. Only about one in ten Falcons are sold "stripped," a Ford man reports. A Chicago dealer who averages about 150 Falcon sales a month, adds that "50 per cent of our sales are for the car with the de luxe interior. The people are not looking for the real stripped car."

Fingers Crossed

Used-car dealers may be in for some rough sledding. The expectation is that competition from the compacts will drive down prices of the older autos. That has already happened in some places. Frank Taylor Ford, Los Angeles's biggest used-car dealer, estimates prices have been cut an average of $100 since the Falcon came out. Most say they haven't yet been hurt. But, admits Atlanta's Ernest G. Beaudry, Inc., "we're keeping our fingers crossed."

Foreign-car makers are also eyeing the compacts closely. They built themselves a lucrative market in the U.S. as sales soared from 160,000 to close to 600,000 in a decade. They now account for 10 per cent of all the cars sold in the U.S. At least 60 different foreign makes now compete for the U.S. dollar, although a few brands dominate the market:

• Volkswagen—which sold 104,000 cars in the first eleven months of 1959.

• Renault's Dauphine—sales in America: 82,000.

• English Ford—39,000.

• GM's German-built Opel—36,000.

• Italy's Fiat—35,000.

• France's Simca (partly Chrysler-owned)—33,000.

Will the foreign cars be able to hold onto their U.S. market?

Detroit doesn't think so. "Imported cars . . . will likely drop to about 7 per cent [of the market] in 1960," says Ford's Wright. The importers disagree. They think the new entries will simply widen the appeal for all small cars. A Detroit dealer selling Swedish Volvos and Saabs, for example, said: "When compact cars came out we did much better than we'd done before. The Big Three, coming out with their small cars, put the seal of approval on them."

Jack C. Kent, sales manager for Renault in the U.S., agreed. "In our own minds," he said, "we feel the U.S. compact cars have stirred interest in the Dauphine." Kent also feels sure that the foreign cars will hang onto as much as 11 per cent of the U.S. market—but he is just as certain that as many as 40 of the 60-odd imported makes now selling will fade away before long.

But even if some makes fade, the compact car, in one form or another, promises to be around for a long while. American Motors' George Romney predicts flatly that by 1963 more than half of all U.S. cars sold will be compacts.

Hollywood's Move Toward Mature Films

By William K. Zinsser

In the following selection from a February 1960 issue of *Life* magazine, William K. Zinsser discusses the advent of new movies that depart from the light entertainment that characterized the Hollywood films of the previous decades. He observes that movies released at the start of 1960 such as *Anatomy of a Murder, The Best of Everything, A Summer Place*, and *It Started with a Kiss* have started a trend that a Catholic official has berated as "a sex binge." Zinsser warns that more adult movies are being shot during the rest of the year, including *Butterfield 8, The Apartment*, and *Lolita*.

According to Zinsser, many movie producers and writers welcome the shift as it signals new artistic freedom and the opportunity for both artists and audiences to gain maturity. Among the general public, however, there are cries of alarm. While the Production Code of the Motion Picture Association of America sets limits on what could be shown on the screen, Zinsser suggests that a classification system, similar to that being enforced in Europe, might be helpful to assuage public concern. He concludes that, in the long run, parents will be ultimately responsible for keeping impressionable youngsters from more adult-themed movies. William K. Zinsser wrote for *Life*.

Many parents . . . who take their children to the current hit, *Anatomy of a Murder*, are embarrassed to find that the movie busies itself less with anatomy than physiology. In its reconstruction of a rape case it uses words that are clinical, to say the least. The crucial clue is nothing so trite as a gun or a purse but rather a pair of panties that had vanished from the scene.

The Best of Everything and *A Summer Place* deal not only with unmarried young people faced with pregnancy but also with their adulterous elders, proving, if nothing else, that the different generations have some interests in common after all. *Blue Denim* also involves a girl well this side of voting age who gets with child. As in *The Best of Everything*, there is talk of visiting the kindly old abortionist. *It Started with a Kiss* seeks its laugh in the notion that a bride would hold her bridegroom at bay for a month to prove that he did not marry her for the wrong reason—an embargo that drives him to cold showers and other desperate measures.

The result of these and other candid movies has been a cry of alarm heard round the land. One Protestant leader deplored Hollywood's emphasis on "sex for sex's sake," and a Roman Catholic monsignor chided the film industry for going on "a sex binge." Citizens assail the movie capital with huffy letters. Trade newspapers have fretted over the problem at great length, and quite a few state legislatures, for their part, are pondering stiffer film censorship laws. But the reaction takes no simple organized form. It consists, instead, of a general awareness that American movies have suddenly become more "frank," "adult" or "dirty," that the public morality may somehow be in danger, and that perhaps something ought to be done about it.

Eye-Opening Schedule

But if the populace is aroused now, it hasn't seen anything yet. The production schedule for the months ahead bodes a full diet of films that would not have been permitted even a year ago. Two of John O'Hara's most libido-centered novels, *Butterfield 8* and *From the Terrace*, are now being shot. Director Billy Wilder's new film, *The Apartment*, is the story of a young man who rises swiftly in his firm by lending his apartment to his bosses for their dalliance after the working day. Richard Zanuck's next movie will be *The Chapman Report*, which tells of a team of researchers investigating the sex habits of the American woman. *Home from the Hill, Strangers When We Meet* and *The Fugitive Kind* center on adultery. Jack Kerouac's *The Subterraneans* will paint the many faces of sex among the beatniks, and even *Lolita* will go into production this spring. Stanley Kubrick will direct the filming of Vladimir Nabokov's wildly controversial novel about an older man and a 12-year-old girl touring the country motels together. . . .

The cries of alarm are bound to grow louder in 1960. There will be demands for censorship and for a system of classifying movies "for adults only." Neither of these cures is likely to work. For though the problem may seem to be a simple case of morality *vs.* immorality, it involves many subtle factors. The new freedom is more than a revolution within the film industry itself. It is part of a change in the entertainment appetites of the nation as a whole.

Obviously the new freedom raises grave dangers. Liberty breeds license, and parents will need sharp eyes to distinguish between mature films and merely salacious ones. On the other hand, the new freedom could bring benefits. It could mean that Hollywood, long accused of catering to "the 12-year-old mind," will at last have a chance to grow up. The American movie audience, which has sheepishly accepted 12-year-old fare, may grow up in the bargain. The aim is laudable. Whether it can be realized will depend on the good taste and judgment of both movie-maker and movie-goer.

Motives Behind the Trend

The main reason for making films that are called more adult is, of course, to attract more adults. Television has replaced movies as the family medium, and Hollywood's only hope of wooing grown men and women into the theaters is to give them something that they cannot see on TV at home. "People no longer go to 'the movies.'" [Alfred] Hitchcock says, "they go to an event." This event can be any number of things: a movie so big, like *Ben-Hur*, that only a theater screen will hold it, or a film in which appropriate smells are piped at the spectators. But such projects are expensive and rare, and instead of relying on technical tricks to win the adult trade, Hollywood would prefer to seek new themes and characters.

Nor is money the only motive. Many good directors and writers feel that their art can never grow if it is hobbled by outmoded taboos. They are bursting to try fresh ideas on the screen and to achieve the freedoms that the theater enjoys. The success of foreign films in America has, needless to say, been a persuasive lesson. It is true that some of these films, notably those starring Brigitte Bardot, have prospered for reasons that are not strictly esthetic. Bardot's Law, or box-office strength through nudity, has proved almost as infallible as the law of gravity. But many other imported films, such as those directed by Ingmar Bergman, have triumphed on sheer artistic merit. There is no law that says only the Swedes can manage this feat.

If serious movie-makers are eager to mature, so are serious movie fans. Millions of Americans stopped going to motion pictures in the past decade, not so much because TV exerted a rival pull as because what they saw on the movie screen held no reality. The vapid old boy-and-girl plots, tailored by habit to a family trade that no longer existed, contained few ingredients that people could either recognize as honest everyday realism or respond to as stylized but provocative drama.

"Art should help us digest and understand our own experience," says Elia Kazan. "The issue is not one of making immoral movies. Our problem is to prevent moral values from being oversimplified. People see a film that has a phony happy ending, and they get a distorted view which hurts them later. They expect life to be what it isn't.". . .

The Production Code

Hollywood movie-makers feel free to tackle almost any subject, though their freedom is not absolute. They are subject to certain obvious controls, such as the laws of obscenity and libel. Above all, however, they submit voluntarily to a body of ethics known as the Production Code of the Motion Picture Association of America. This document, more than anything else, governs what can and cannot be done on the U.S. movie screen. . . .

The Code has a long list of specific taboos. It forbids mercy killings, white slavery, cruelty to animals, vulgar phrases, blasphemous talk, obscene dances and complete nudity as well as indecent overexposure. Unhappily for the enforcers of the Code, many of these "don'ts" are founded on variable standards. One man's obscene dance, for example, is another man's art. . . .

This Code censorship which the industry imposes on itself is the only effective kind remaining in the country at large. Only five states—New York, Maryland, Kansas, West Virginia and Pennsylvania—still have boards to precensor movies. Many other states had such boards in the past but have abolished them. Authorities in certain cities, empowered by municipal laws to protect the community from sin, snip capriciously at incoming films. This practice has resulted in some curious excisions. Boston's censor cut the word "bawdyhouse" from Laurence Olivier's *Henry V* in 1946—but only for Sunday performances and children's matinees. Lloyd T. Binford, who was nearing 90 when he retired as city censor of Memphis a few years ago, banned Ingrid Bergman's movies after she married Roberto Rossellini. He also deleted all train robbery sequences because in his youth he had been on a train that was held up. . . .

Two recent Supreme Court decisions [have hastened] the fall of censorship. The first of these rulings, in 1952, dealt with *The Miracle*, a film that New York State had banned as "sacrilegious." The court overruled the ban, claiming that such terms as "sacrilege" are too vague to be enforced. It also ruled—and this was the revolutionary clause—that the screen is entitled to all the constitutional freedoms guaranteed to the press and other communications media.

The second decision, last June, applied to a film version of *Lady Chatterley's Lover*, which New York State had banned because it stated the unpopular idea that adultery under certain circumstances may be justified. In upsetting the ban, the Supreme Court declared that "the First Amendment's basic guarantee is of freedom to advocate ideas. Its guarantee is not confined to the expression of ideas that are conventional or shared by the majority. It protects advocacy of the opinion that adultery may sometimes be proper, no less than advocacy of socialism or the single tax. The State has thus struck at the very heart of constitutionally protected liberty."

With these two decisions the screen has won almost total freedom, and from now on state censors will have a hard time finding legal grounds for banning a film. This does not mean that a movie cannot be seized or censored after it opens if it violates some existing statute. Nor does it mean that theater owners are required to book films of which they disapprove. But neither of these forms of "delayed" censorship is very common.

One solution frequently proposed is "classification," a routine system in England, France, Italy and other European countries. The British Board of Film Censors, for example, divides all films into three categories: "X"—adults only, "A"—children may attend only if accompanied by an adult, and "U"—suitable for all. In West Germany roughly 40% of all movies are forbidden to children under 16, and in France the minimum age for seeing many films is 18. These films generally include the more amatory French products, like *The Lovers*, which the merest toddler can see legally in the United States.

Would Rating Work?

Would classification work in America? . . .

Champions of classification say that it is bound to come. They feel that there is no other way to let Hollywood make mature films and still protect the morals of minors. Perhaps it will come, but it is not just around the corner.

Meanwhile a few other safeguards are available to worried parents. Religious groups wield varying degrees of control. By far the most effective is the National Legion of Decency, official agency of the Roman Catholic Church in the United States for appraising moral values of films. The Legion's ratings are published in a biweekly list, which is posted in all Catholic churches and schools and is reprinted in most Catholic papers. The main ratings are: "A-1"—morally unobjectionable for all, "A-2"—morally unobjectionable for adults and adolescents, "A-3"—morally unobjectionable for adults, "B"—morally objectionable in part for all, "C"—condemned. . . .

No such unity binds Protestants or Jews in America. Protestant ministers occasionally denounce a movie, but as a group they are not equipped to scold bad films or encourage new ones. The Protestant Motion Picture Council reviews many movies, and these reviews appear in some newspapers and church bulletins. But Protestants are reluctant to make specific recommendations. "We don't want to curb artistry in movies by legislative censorship," says the Rev. Dr. S.F. Mack, head of the National Council of Protestant Churches' Broadcasting and Film Commission. "Any type of censorship is obnoxious to us. We much prefer the regulation of self-choice. It is this human choice, after all, that is the basis of our religion." The Jewish faith also does not have a system for reviewing movies on moral grounds, though they are equally concerned about the problem. They do have agencies, such as the Anti-Defamation League, which guard against the unfavorable depiction of Jewish people on the screen. . . .

Beyond that, there are at least half a dozen periodicals—i.e., *Parents Magazine, The Christian Herald, The Clubwoman*—which regularly rate films on their fitness for different age groups. There is also a monthly journal called *The Green Sheet*, which presents the composite motion picture opinion of 11 social and religious groups, including the American Jewish Committee, the General Federation of Women's Clubs, and the National Congress of Parents and Teachers. This bulletin, issued by the Film Estimate Board, 28 W. 44 St., New York, grades new movies in five age categories.

Parental Guidance

With formal censorship reduced to such a degree, Hollywood enters the 1960s with the best chance it has ever had to reach maturity. All the old watchdogs are losing—or at least loosening—their bite. The Code and the churches are more liberal than ever before, and so are the times. Film censorship has been declared largely unconstitutional, and where censors do survive, they are regarded as somewhat un-American. Classification is still only a distant dream.

This means that the task of policing American movies in the coming era of frank expression will lie in two places. The first is Hollywood itself, for if the motion picture industry misuses its freedom, public opinion will soon snatch that freedom away. But in the last analysis there is only one effective film censor in the United States today, and his job is getting more difficult by the hour. That censor, of course, is every parent. True censorship, like charity, begins at home, the one place where it incontestably belongs.

Lady Chatterley's Lover and Changing Attitudes Toward Literary Censorship

By Arthur Marwick

In his 1998 book, *The Sixties*, Arthur Marwick, professor of history at Open University, notes several trends in the late fifties and early sixties that allowed the appearance of daring, formerly banned works like D.H. Lawrence's *Lady Chatterley's Lover.* First, a new crop of novels which dealt with sex more explicitly was being published. Second, the relaxation of literary censorship enabled the publication of new risqué works as well as the republication and circulation of previously banned ones. And third, both new and old works were appearing in paperback editions for mass markets. Marwick argues that the new novels were liberating. They violated traditional morality by making illicit couplings central to the plot and introducing activities that were previously considered taboo. For *Lady Chatterley's Lover*, the freedom to be republished in America (in an unexpurgated version) came after a New York State court battle in which the 1928 novel was declared not to be mere pornography. The U.S. government appealed the case, but a U.S. Court of Appeals upheld the New York ruling in March 1960, defending Lawrence's work as "a major and distinguished novel." Marwick, who established the Sixties Research Group, is the author of *The Nature of History, Beauty in History*, and *British Society Since 1945.*

Arthur Marwick, *The Sixties: Cultural Revolution in Britain, France, Italy, and the United States.* Oxford: Oxford University Press, 1998. Copyright © 1998 by Oxford University Press. Reproduced by permission.

Three slightly different trends were very apparent in both America and Britain in the final years of the fifties and early sixties: a number of new novels were published which were perceived by contemporaries as being franker and more daring in the way they dealt with sexual matters, while at almost the same time (if anything, the former development came first) changes in literary censorship made possible not only a continuation and exaggeration of the trend but also the publication and circulation of older books which had previously been banned as subverting public morality; the third trend was that both kinds of book (which if confined to limited hardback editions might not have excited the authorities too much) were appearing in paperback for a mass market—for the sixties 'paperback revolution' had already begun. . . .

In America an important criterion was whether a book was pure enough to be sent through the post, thus giving the American post office an important role; essentially decisions lay in the hands of the courts, depending upon how they interpreted the first amendment guaranteeing freedom of speech. A case of 1955–57 established that the notion that 'redeeming social importance' might be used as a defence, and indeed this was the defence used in the 1957 trial in San Francisco of Allen Ginsberg's *Howl.* Deciding that it too would make use of this defence, Grove Press of New York brought out an unexpurgated edition of *Lady Chatterley's Lover* in the spring of 1959, when it was at once challenged by the post office: 'If this book is not filth', asked the postmaster-general, 'pray tell me what filth is.' The book was duly banned, but Grove Press took immediate counteraction to restrain the postmaster-general from preventing distribution. In the US District Court, Southern District of New York, Judge Bryan ruled on 21 July 1959 that *Lady Chatterley* could be shipped through the mails, noting: 'the record . . . indicates general acceptance of the book', and concluding:

> These trends appear in all media of public expression, in the kind of language used and the subjects discussed in polite society, in pictures, advertisements and dress, and in other ways familiar to see. Today such things are generally tolerated whether we approve or not.

This is the argument which is applied also in film censorship: people's attitudes are changing, thus the interpretation of censorship must change also. It is a self-reinforcing process, of course: people become more open, more explicit, less ashamed, less clandestine, in what they read and watch and in what they do; relaxation in censorship, greater daring in the materials available to them, legitimizes the changes in behaviour, and encourages further development towards freedom and permissiveness.

Stirrings of Change

However, the fact that we are still only in the period of first stirrings of change is driven home by the way in which the battle continued to rage backwards and forwards well into the early sixties. The American government immediately appealed against Bryan's ruling. However, the US Court of Appeals, declaring on 26 March 1960: 'this is a major and distinguished novel, and Lawrence one of the great writers of the age', upheld what may be termed Bryan's historic judgment. Certainly those American magazines which fifteen months earlier had identified the power of the teenager were now preoccupied with the significance for public morality of the *Lady Chatterley* case. Grove Press had marketed the book at an expensive $6, but several other publishing outfits immediately jumped in with extremely cheap editions, including that of the Tabloid Publishing Company in New England which brought out an edition in newspaper format for selling on street corners at 25 cents: thus did the decisions of elevated lawgivers run straight to the hearts and minds of the general public.

It was in the latter half of 1959 that Penguin Books, an infinitely more reputable and respectable organization than any of the American ones just mentioned, decided to mark the thirtieth anniversary (falling on the following year) of Lawrence's death, and the twenty-fifth of Penguin's birth, with eight Lawrence titles, including an unexpurgated *Lady Chatterley's Lover*. Of this, 200,000 copies were printed, but held back while a dozen topics were sent to the Director of Public Prosecutions. Although the DPP had recently decided, in some recognition of the changing attitudes to which I have referred several times, not to prosecute the British edition of [Vladimir Nabokov's novel] *Lolita*, brought out by Weidenfeld and Nicolson in 1959, he did decide to prosecute the Lawrence which, in contrast to the elegant euphemisms of Nabokov was loaded with the four-letter words which sections of the British public found deliriously exciting in print, but which

by a widely accepted convention were held to be beyond the pale
of civilized life. Thus it came to pass that the most celebrated and
illuminating show trial of this critical time of change, was held
at the Old Bailey during five days in November 1960. . . .

The jury (five of whom had had difficulty in just reading the
oath) acquitted *Lady Chatterley* of obscenity; printing hundreds
of thousands of new copies (two million were sold within the
year), Penguin added a blurb referring triumphantly to the trial:
'it was not just a legal tussle, but a conflict of generation and
class.' A new openness about class, together with actual changes
in class relationships are critical aspects of the sixties. For the
moment I want to concentrate on the way in which the content
of newly published novels was changing, particularly in the
United States, where a new kind of explicitness was rather more
evident, and came earlier, than was the case in Britain.

New Emphasis on Details

Novels could be 'liberated' (and 'liberating', my argument in part
is—though the censors and the censorious were still saying
'pornographic') in two ways. First, they could integrate into the
narrative behaviour and acts which violated traditional morality.
Beyond question, sexual relations outside marriage, illegitimate
births, and so on were not new in literature, and certainly fea-
tured quite prominently in the works of novelists established well
before the late fifties—Graham Greene and Somerset Maugham,
for instance, not to mention, say, Colette in France or Moravia
in Italy. But there could be quite a difference with regard to the
amount of emphasis placed on illicit couplings, or their central-
ity to the plot; more, there could be the introduction of activities
that had previously remained largely taboo—sex with an under-
age girl (as in *Lolita*); sex between teenagers; sex between blacks
and whites; sex as a completely casual and/or joyful activity
(without the portentousness that traditionally had to be associated with it); homosexual (and bisexual) activities; masturbation
(female as well as male); oral sex, anal sex, and sex described by
a woman, from a woman's point of view, often dispassionately,
or (most shocking of all) humorously; the comedy, and the
magic, of tumescence and detumescence, in nipples as well as
genitals, and from all angles.

Secondly (and this was really the more critical feature), there
could be much more detailed, explicit (and therefore potentially

arousing) descriptions of these activities, perhaps, though not necessarily, employing some of the taboo words. Nineteenth-century novelists might take you to the bedroom door, but no further: twentieth-century novelists certainly went further, but did not usually go into detail. All sorts of daring things had been done before by isolated and banned authors like D.H. Lawrence and Henry Miller; though the defence steered clear of it, and the prosecution failed to perceive it, *Lady Chatterley's Lover* did in fact contain an explicit scene of buggery; in Henry Miller sex was not only almost continuous, but presented in lavish detail; what was new in the later fifties was that this kind of material was entering into a considerable number of mainstream novels, and was being integrated into straightforward accounts of recognizable everyday life. (Miller's characters were bohemians and drop-outs; *Lady Chatterley*, as everyone knows, is simply an everyday story of aristocrats and their gamekeepers.) There was a totally new emphasis on genitalia, their mechanics, functions, and the exact sensations they produce.

U-2 Spy Plane Pilot Is Interrogated in Moscow

By the *Los Angeles Times*

On May 1, 1960, an American U-2 reconnaissance plane was brought down while flying over Soviet territory. The pilot, Francis Gary Powers, was captured and interrogated by the Russians. The Soviets released part of that interrogation to the world press to embarrass the United States, which, at that time, was supposedly working to improve peaceful relations with Russia. In the interview, excerpted below, Powers admits to flying over Soviet space, gathering intelligence information, and being under contract with the Central Intelligence Agency. The U-2 incident caused a chill in the relations between the United States and the Soviet Union. It eventually led Russian premier Nikita Khrushchev to cancel U.S.-Soviet talks at the Paris Summit on May 16. Powers was subsequently convicted by the Russians of espionage, but the Soviet Union released him and allowed him to return home to his country twenty months later—and only after grueling negotiations with the United States.

LONDON, May 14—Radio Moscow broadcast today extracts of what it called an interrogation of Francis G. Powers, American pilot of the U-2 plane shot down May 1 over Russia.

The text as received in London by the British Broadcasting Corp.:

Pleading Guilty

Question: Is the accusation brought against you clear?

Answer: Yes, it is.

Q: Do you plead guilty?

A: I plead guilty to the fact that I have flown over Soviet territory and over the points indicated on the chart, turned on and off the necessary controls of the special equipment mounted aboard my plane that I consider was being done with the aim of collecting intelligence information about the USSR.

Q: Tell us with more details what you plead guilty to.

A: In accordance with the contract which was signed by me with the CIA (Central Intelligence Agency) of the U.S.A., I am pilot of the special air detachment of the U.S.A. dealing with the collection of information about operational radio stations and radar on the territory of the USSR and, as I suppose, about locations of rockets. Our air detachment is permanently located at the U.S. Turkish air base, Incirlik, near Adana City, Turkey. I have been serving in this detachment since August 1956 and each year for several times flew in special high-altitude plane U-2 along the borders of the USSR with Turkey, Iran and Afghanistan. Besides, in 1956–57 I performed three or four flights over the Black Sea without crossing the state borders of the USSR. It is difficult for me to recollect the numbers of such flights, but I flew repeatedly.

During these flights the special equipment mounted on my plane took bearings of the signals of Soviet radio stations and radar. In any case I was told so and given such assignments but I cannot say exactly whether the equipment of my plane took the bearings of the mentioned stations and installations, as I am not familiar with the equipment and I was never told about the results of my work. Before such flights we were instructed and told over which points during the flight we should turn on and off the controls of the corresponding equipment.

Q: At what altitude did you fly when your plane was shot down?

A: At the altitude of 68,000 ft.

Whom Do You Work For?

Q: What reward were you supposed to receive for today's flight?

A: None. I receive a salary of about $2,400 per month for carrying out those tasks which I have to fulfill. My today's task was to fly from Pakistan to Norway.

Q: Where do you serve?

A: From 1956 I served in the U.S. Air Force but at present I work at an American office.

Q: What is the name of the office?

A: This is a combination of Civil Aviation and Air Force Service. All this is disguised and coded under the name "Unit 10-10."

Q: What are the tasks of this unit?

A: The main task of this unit is to locate the radio stations in action and the rocket-launching sites.

Q: What is Col. (Shelton)?

A: He is commander of this unit.

Q: What sort of a unit is it?

A: It deals with the collection of military information.

The Pill Raises Hopes and Fears

By *Time*

The following article, taken from a 1967 issue of *Time*, notes that when oral contraceptives were first introduced in the United States in May 1960, they held the promise of liberating the sex and family life of a large segment of the U.S. population. By 1965, the U.S. National Fertility Study showed that of all white American women using any form of contraception, 24 percent were on the pill. The pill particularly had become popular among married women who wanted to postpone pregnancies until they were more prepared to raise a family.

The pill also had an impact on the rest of the world, especially developing nations saddled with overpopulation and poverty. In Latin America, the pill brought deliverance to women and their families who could not otherwise feed and nurture five or six children. The same has been true for impoverished women in America. All was not good news, though. Groups whose religions oppose the use of "artificial" contraceptives were faced with a moral dilemma. Catholics, for one, had been asked to rely on their conscience. Another issue raised against the pill was its effect on the unmarried, especially young people, who might feel a greater freedom to engage in sex.

"The pill" is a miraculous tablet that contains as little as one thirty-thousandth of an ounce of chemical. It costs 1¼¢ to manufacture; a month's supply now sells for $2.00 retail. It is little more trouble to take on schedule than a daily vitamin. Yet in a mere six years it has changed and liberated the sex and family life of a large and still growing segment of the U.S. population: eventually, it promises to do the same for much of the world. . . .

The pills were first approved for prescription use in the U.S. in [May] 1960. Now [in 1967], there are twelve varieties, divided into two main classes, but all have two principal effects. First, they regularize a woman's monthly cycle so that she has her "period" every 26 to 28 days, as nature presumably intended. To this extent, the pills are biologically normalizing. Their second major effect is to do something that nature neither intended nor foresaw, and that is to prevent the release of a fertilizable egg from the woman's ovaries during the cycle in which the pills are taken, and thus make it impossible for her to conceive. . . .

"Pincus Pills"

Physiologist Gregory Pincus of the Worcester Foundation for Experimental Biology and gynecologist John Rock of Harvard University rate high among the pioneers of oral contraception. It was at Harvard, too, that Dr. Fuller Albright noted in the mid-1940s that an excess of estrogen in the bloodstream soon after the end of menstruation somehow prevented ovulation. A few years later, Pincus and Rock were working together to find a way of helping subfertile women ovulate, and thus conceive. They first had to regularize the woman's cycle, and they hit upon a synthetic progestin chemically akin to another female sex hormone, progesterone. The progestin, taken for 20 days in mid-menstrual cycle, suppressed ovulation by simulating pregnancy. Taken off the medicine, the women had a more normal cycle, with surer ovulation. After Pincus and Rock had produced a gratifying number of conceptions, a new idea struck them: Why not use the progestin deliberately to suppress ovulation every month—in other words, as a contraceptive?

At first the drug worked well. Several days after a woman stopped taking it, she had what seemed like a normal but mild menstrual period. There were few side effects. But as the drug was further purified, Dr. Rock began to hear patients complain of too much "breakthrough bleeding" in mid-cycle. Analysis showed that the purified drug contained no detectable estrogen. Apparently estrogen, even in the most minute quantity, prevented some side effects, including unwanted bleeding. So when

Chicago's G.D. Searle & Co., which had worked closely with Pincus and Rock, began making "the Pincus pills" as Enovid in 1957, the formulation contained 66 parts progestin to one part estrogen. The progestin dose has been reduced by as much as 90% in Searle's newest pills, Ovulen, but the combination principle is the same.

Other hormone investigators took a different direction, concentrating on the rediscovered, though still not fully understood, powers of estrogen. From the fifth to the 20th day of a normal woman's cycle, her estrogen level is fairly steady, except for a dip at the time of ovulation. If they could prevent this dip, the researchers reasoned, they could prevent ovulation. They felt it would be more natural to do this by providing nothing but added estrogen until the 20th day, and then giving progestin only briefly. San Antonio Researcher Dr. Joseph W. Goldzeiher worked with Syntex Laboratories to develop the resulting "sequentials." Beginning with Day 5, the woman takes a white estrogen pill for 15 days, then a distinctively colored progestin (with a protective smidgen of estrogen added) for five or six days. The sequentials, like the combinations, tend to regularize the cycle, and most women who take them have an acceptably mild menstrual period.

Skipped a Day

All the pills of both types now approved by the Food and Drug Administration for U.S. prescription are as close to 100% effective as any medication ever devised for any purpose. When a woman "on the pills" has become pregnant, it has been shown in virtually every case—and suspected in the others—that she has skipped a pill or two. The failure rate is slightly higher on the sequentials, apparently because the estrogen taken early in the cycle wears off rapidly, and a single day's missed pill may spell pregnancy. The progestin combinations afford a slightly broader margin of safety.

Like all other potent medicines, the pills produce many incidental effects. Some are good, some bad. . . .

The side effect most commonly complained of is weight gain—up to 20 lbs., say some women. Yet most gynecologists believe this was caused only by early, high-dosage forms, and that today's one-milligram pills rarely provoke a gain of more than five pounds. The sequentials usually cause less weight gain than the combinations. The next most frequent complaints are nausea ("like being four months pregnant"), breast tenderness and break-through bleeding. These usually disappear within three months.

Despite dark fears, there is not a shred of evidence that the pills cause cancer. In fact, they may even give some protection against it. But because estrogens are believed to promote the growth of some breast and cervical cancers, the pills may not be prescribed for women who are known or suspected to have this type of disease. Similarly, there is no evidence that the pills caused blood clots that might travel to the lungs or develop in the brain. But for safety's sake, they are not prescribed for women with any history of clotting problems. . . .

For every American woman who has rejected the pills because of conscious doubt or unconscious fears and guilt, a dozen have accepted them. Says Dr. Richard Frank, medical chief of Chicago's Planned Parenthood clinics: "More than five million women can't be wrong about the acceptability of the pills." This impressive total, according to the 1965 National Fertility Study,

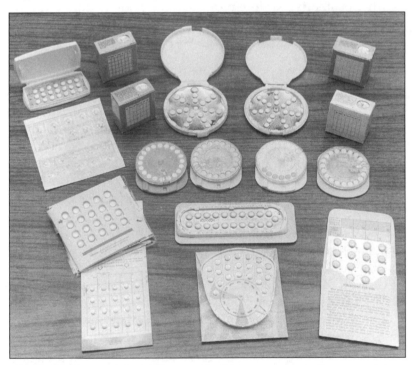

The development of the birth control pill gave women more control over their bodies and their futures.

means that of all white American women using any form of contraception, 24% are on the pills. . . .

For married couples whose religious beliefs interpose no moral problem, the pill is indeed a boon. . . .

Four Little Indians

Typical of the woman who has had all the children she wants and dreads that "menopause baby" is an Atlanta mother of three, aged 44, who says: "I'm getting too old to start looking after another baby. I've been taking the pill for almost two years with no side effects, and it's much simpler than any other method I've tried." To the neurotics who complain that it is too difficult or too much trouble to take a pill a day, a 34-year-old mother in Oak Park, Michigan, responds: "I have my hands full running after four little Indians, and if I had another I'd die. The mere thought of having an unwanted baby is enough to make me remember to take my pills."

The pill is equally helpful to the newly married who want babies at times of their choosing. Says a Detroit secretary: "Sex is especially important when you first get married, and it was so much easier not to have to worry about having a baby that first year." An Indiana teacher, 23, concurs: "When I got married I was still in college, and I wanted to be certain that I finished. Now we want to buy a home, and it's going to be possible a lot sooner if I teach. With the pill I know I can keep earning money and not worry about an accident that would ruin everything." For all these women, the pill spells freedom from fear.

Catholics and Conscience

The pill poses two grave moral problems. The first affects Roman Catholics and, for different theological reasons, the smaller number of Orthodox Jews. Not until 1930 did the Vatican modify the Augustinian rule that sex must be for procreation, when Pope Pius XI approved the rhythm method. The Vatican has banned all mechanical and chemical contraception. But Dr. Rock, an unswerving Catholic, has been arguing ever since he sired the pill that its use imitates nature—which occasionally, but only occasionally, makes a woman skip ovulation—and that it should therefore be approved by the Vatican.

Pope Paul said last October [1966] that the question of birth control was not open to doubt. But the Rev. Albert Schlitzer, head of Notre Dame's theology department, declares: "Many Catholics believe that there is still doubt, so it remains a personal choice. A good many theologians would question whether it is a matter of divine law at all. Many Catholics have already made up their minds, and will follow their decisions no matter what the Pope says in the future."

What Paul will say and even when he will say it are still the subject of speculation. In his encyclical [in 1967] the Pope said: "It is for the parents to decide, with full knowledge of the matter, on the number of their children. . . . In this they must follow the demands of their own conscience enlightened by God's law authentically interpreted." Dr. Rock interpreted it his way: "Oh, perfect! Parental responsibility and the supremacy of conscience—that's an excellent way to satisfy the Old Guard as well as the young." The Old Guard was unmoved. Said Msgr. William F. McManus, director of the Family Life Bureau in the Archdiocese of New York: "I see in the encyclical no substantial change in what the Vatican has said for some time in the matter of family control.". . .

"It Takes Character"

The second moral problem posed by the pills relates to the unmarried. Does the convenient contraceptive promote promiscuity? In some cases, no doubt it does—as did the automobile, the drive-in movie and the motel. But the consensus among both physicians and sociologists is that a girl who is promiscuous on the pill would have been promiscuous without it. The more mature of the unmarried in the Now Generation say that, far from promoting promiscuity, the pills impose a sense of responsibility. Formerly, many a young woman rejected premarital relations specifically because of her fear of pregnancy. Now, on the pills, she has to make the decision according to her own conscience. . . .

At the high school level it is harder to separate contraception from sexual delinquency, and the lack of it from pregnancy and possible abortion. Once a teen-ager has become pregnant, has been expelled from school, and has had either a baby or an abortion, the chances are that she will soon be pregnant again. To break the pattern, Dr. Philip Sarrel recently took 90 pregnancy dropouts in New Haven [Connecticut], set up special classes for them and, with their parents' permission, put them on the pill or gave them IUDs. On form, he could have expected 50 pregnancies within a year and a half. Actually there was only one—and that because a girl deliberately skipped her pills. In Baltimore, a preventive pill-and-IUD program is being carried out among pubertal-age girls in "high-risk" (slum) areas. . . .

Health on Wheels

When Searle first marketed Enovid in 1960, it cost $11 for a month's supply, automatically limiting its use. Today, with mass production, smaller doses and intense competition, the pills are cheap enough to be dispensed to hundreds of thousands of women, either at nominal cost or at no cost, through clinics operated by Planned Parenthood and some public agencies.

One of the most effective programs is a Planned Parenthood operation in Birmingham, Alabama, called Health on Wheels. The brainchild of Planned Parenthood Chairman Tom Bolding, its wheels are those of a Dodge van with its own generator. Equipped with examining table and the latest medical equipment, staffed by a nurse and a doctor who volunteers for a day's duty, the van takes the back roads into remote parts of Winston and Walker counties. . . .

Even in areas where poverty and population pressure are greatest, the pill is beginning to crowd the IUD. Dr. Rice-Wray, now in Mexico City, pooh-poohs the idea that poor, illiterate women cannot learn to take pills regularly: "We have some women who've been on the pills for eight years straight, and we can't get 'em off them—not even to take part in our study of a once-a-month injection.". . .

Latin America counts 2,000,000 pill users, a remarkably large number considering its Roman Catholic heritage and low income levels. But that is still less than 5% of the fertile women. Among the masses, baby follows baby with such deadly rapidity that Colombian women crouch on the ground to abort themselves with sharp sticks. In Chile, the victims of bungled abortions occupy 20% of the beds in maternity wards and use up 27% of the transfusion blood. . . . About one-sixth of Chile's fertile women now have IUDs or take the pills. Next week, partly in recognition of this progress, Chile will be host to the eighth world conference of the International Planned Parenthood Federation.

At the conference, talk will turn from what present contraceptives are achieving to new methods still in the experimental stage, which it is hoped will eventually surpass the pill in simplicity and effectiveness.

Anti-HUAC Demonstrations Focus on Civil Liberties and World Peace

By Massimo Teodori

In the following selection, author Massimo Teodori relates the significance of the student protest against the House Un-American Activities
Committee (HUAC) held in May 1960 in San Francisco. The demonstrations signaled the birth of student dissent on the issues of civil liberties at home and peace in the world. HUAC, a government body established in 1938, was a watchdog organization designed to protect
America from political subversion. Continuing through the fifties and
sixties, HUAC investigated subversive activities and propaganda
waged by local and foreign groups and often treated political dissenters
as criminals. The student activists argued that HUAC violated the same
civil liberties it professed to protect. HUAC's powers constituted an ex-
treme form of censorship and threatened the ideals of free thought and
expression. Apart from HUAC's totalitarian ways, other concerns gal-
vanized students into political action—the continuous preparation for
war, the escalating arms race, the launch of more atomic tests, and the
Cuba problem. The protests did not defeat HUAC. The organization

Massimo Teodori, *The New Left: A Documentary History*. Indianapolis: The Bobbs-Merrill Company, 1969. Copyright © 1969 by Massimo Teodori. All rights reserved. Reproduced by permission of Scribner, an imprint of Simon & Schuster Adult Publishing Group.

lasted until 1969 when it was renamed and reorganized as the Internal Security Committee. Six years later, that department was abolished.

Teodori is the editor of *The New Left: A Documentary History*, a 1969 anthology that is the source of this essay. He taught at the University of Rome and held a political science fellowship at the University of California at Berkeley.

As was the case in the South, the causes which determined the birth of dissent and protest in the rest of the country were, at the beginning of the 1960s, limited in nature and strictly related to issues of individual liberties or to specific policies of the administration. Students began to stir on campuses and in the streets, not in the name of an alternative political vision or a revolutionary strategy, but for essentially liberal and humanistic motives. Their political involvement moved from the particular to the general, from moral concern to an analysis of structures. Here, as in the civil-rights struggle, the process of radicalization and the growth of a more general opposition to American society and institutions was slow and gradual, and was due more to the kind of response the movement elicited from the liberal wing of traditional political forces than to the intentions of its participants.

Even though cold-war ideology did not assume the paranoiac aspects of the McCarthy years [when Senator Joseph McCarthy led a crusade against suspected Communists in the 1950s], it still openly and subtly permeated both a foreign policy based on power, with the division of the world into spheres of influence, and the processes of political decision-making domestically. Any evaluation of the rebirth of dissent in America must consider the background of a society which left no room for the development of views different from those considered right for "democracy" and for the "free world." Between 1960 and 1963, the crucial issues around which protest catalyzed and movements organized represented a direct reaction against the systematic cold-war view and concerned two main areas: civil liberties and peace. The 1950s had been particularly conservative with respect to both subjects, and this heredity of conservatism, carried into the next decade, aroused violent opposition.

In May 1960, eight thousand students from the University of California at Berkeley and other Bay Area colleges, together with

habitués of certain cafés in San Francisco's North Beach, fre-
quented by the rebels and artists of the beat generation, held a
demonstration in front of the San Francisco City Hall, where the
House Un-American Activities Committee (HUAC) was meeting to investigate real or supposed communist activity. The
HUAC investigations were imbued with that typical spirit of domestic totalitarianism which caused political dissenters to be
treated as criminals. The function of HUAC (which had been
founded in 1938) was to make from time to time investigations
of (1) the extent, character and objects of un-American propaganda activities in the U.S., (2) the diffusion within the U.S. of
subversive and un-American propaganda that is instigated from
foreign countries or of a domestic origin and attacks the principle of the form of government as guaranteed by our Constitution,
and (3) all other questions in relation thereto that would aid Congress in any necessary remedial legislation. Not only subversive
activity, therefore, but even propaganda was subject to investi-
gation. What the protestors had to deal with was a violation of
those very civil liberties that should have been the most precious
political inheritance of the Western world.

The militant methods of the anti-HUAC demonstration were
to serve as an affirmation of simple liberal objectives, namely,
that a committee which had been established in the prewar period be abolished and that citizens not be persecuted for their political opinions. The students, who had been raised to believe the
myth of the great American democracy, found here—no less than
in other aspects of their life—a contradiction between fact and
principle, between values their upbringing had taught them to
cherish and the exercise of authoritarian power by individuals
who professed those same values. Beyond the specific episode,
that unexpected explosion of physical protest reflected a much
more general state of malaise originating in a conflict between
ideals and reality.

> We came out to demonstrate against the House Committee on
> Un-American Activities, not merely as a defense of our right to
> freedom of thought, but as an affirmation of our duty to think, to
> think socially and independently, to take part as students in the
> community and to take responsibility as students for its direc-
> tion. . . . That morning when we went out to demonstrate against
> the House Committee, we had other things in our mind as well:

capital punishment, integration, peace, and all the issues in which our lives were involved and which we had begun, as students, to think about again.

Opposition to Moral Violence

The spirit of the San Francisco demonstrators was similar to that which, a few months earlier, had motivated Fred Moore, an eighteen-year-old student, to hold a solitary vigil on the Berkeley campus in protest against compulsory military training at a state university. It was similar to the spirit which had provoked a march against capital punishment and against the execution of Caryl Chessman in February of that same year. When society acts with physical and moral violence—persecution of political adversaries, compulsory military indoctrination, and disdain for human life— the first instinct is a moral reaction; deepening the analysis and transforming it into conscious political opposition follows. This developed during the months following the anti-HUAC demonstration, when an attempt was made, by means of a widespread propaganda apparatus, to gain support for the notion that the disorder had been organized by communists. J. Edgar Hoover, head of the FBI, testified that there had been a prearranged plot whose objective was violence. The film *Operation Abolition*, which was to have supported this idea by showing the confrontations between students and police in San Francisco, produced the very opposite effect in the course of a year: it convinced the majority of those students who had borne the brunt of the unwarranted police violence to continue the debate on civil liberties in the universities. Around this theme, committees for the abolition of HUAC were formed according to a method of political organization which became typical of the new movements, i.e., gathering groups of students and nonstudents around single issues, bypassing already existing organizations.

Cuba and the Growth of Dissent

Events in Cuba played an important role in the growth of dissent within the United States. The Cuban revolution, culminating with Castro's seizure of power in January 1959, threatened the division of the world. Just as political dissenters within the United States became national enemies, so in the entire Western world nations and peoples who chose independence from the U.S. could not be tolerated. The principle of self-determination became a value subordinated to power and could in no way be allowed to threaten the established system. President Kennedy would certainly have preferred a "democratic" regime to [Cuban dictator Fulgencio] Batista's allied with the United States, but when faced with the autonomous development of the Cuban revolution, it became legitimate to bring the *heterodox* phenomenon under control.

We do not intend here to discuss the transformation of the Cuban revolution from libertarian and nationalist to communist, nor to discuss the level of political democracy in the present regime. The fact remains that the United States—first through political and economic pressure, followed by the breaking off of diplomatic relations, and then with the organization of the Bay of Pigs invasion in April 1961—followed a policy of maintaining military and economic supremacy and playing the role of international police.

In order to clarify the relationship between the new movement of dissent and traditional liberalism, it is well to remember that it was John F. Kennedy who enacted a policy toward Cuba which one would have thought characteristic of a much more conservative leader, and that it was the men of the New Frontier who first lied about the role played by the CIA and then justified their own lies in the name of *raison d'état* [i.e., for purely political reasons]. Among students, reaction to America's conduct in Cuba once more took on a liberal tone: they formed the Fair Play for Cuba Committee, demanding that the administration take a proper attitude toward the small country and its new regime. The fascination the Cuban revolution held for young people lay precisely in its romantic and humanist character. It seemed to represent the restoration of human action as protagonist of the historical process, in spite of the repressive military and economic apparatus it had to combat, as well as the inflexible international order and the desperate objective conditions of the country. . . .

Support for the revolution grew in direct proportion to the increase of American pressure; visits to Cuba became more frequent as people desired to learn firsthand the facts which authorities attempted to hide by various means, including ban on travel; the violence of the revolution gradually came to be understood and justified, even by pacifists, who judged the guerrillas' action in the contexts of international violence and the perpetuation of poverty in Latin America.

Focus on Peace

The expropriation of resources by the war industry; the maintenance of a permanent state of preparation for all-out war; the atomic testing carried out by both the United States and the Soviet Union—these are the reasons that the youthful protest movement found peace to be one of the most important objectives of the moment.

We have mentioned that the rebellious instinct always springs from moral considerations, particularly in places like the United States, where there were no forces capable of setting off campaigns more fundamentally political in nature. This was also true for the peace movement, which, in its first mass meetings, concentrated on denouncing the horror of atomic warfare, proclaiming the right to live, appealing to governments to stop nuclear testing, and circulating petitions in favor of controlled disarmament. The San Francisco peace march of 1960 was organized as a means of giving the people a voice in the debate on disarmament. . . . The peace movement was based on the moral principle of the right to life. The National Committee for a Sane Nuclear Policy (SANE), around which the movement revolved at first, was guided by a hope of stopping the drift toward war through the banning of atomic weapons, and its propaganda did not extend much beyond appeals for survival and warnings on the danger of an accidental outbreak of nuclear war. The most heterogeneous elements were to be found around the peace movement: liberals willing to participate in single-issue movements; communists who saw in the front ranks of the movement possibilities for action which were otherwise precluded; moral and radical pacifists, religious groups, and democratic socialists. However, it was not these kinds of affiliations which caused the peace movement to grow. It became capable of mobilizing on a wider and more active basis only when the initiative passed into the hands of nonaffiliated students, and the issue of peace held for them the same moral imperatives to action as the civil-rights movement in the South.

ARTICLE 8

The Paris Summit Collapses

By Nikita Khrushchev and Dwight D. Eisenhower

After World War II, the Big Four—the United States, the Soviet Union, France, and Great Britain—had been meeting regularly to discuss increasing Cold War tensions between the Soviets and Western Allies. At the opening of the Big Four Summit in Paris on May 16, 1960, Russian premier Nikita Khrushchev stunned his audience by saying the conference could not continue. He demanded that President Eisenhower of the United States first issue an apology for the incursion of a U.S. spy plane into Soviet air space on May 1. In turn, President Dwight D. Eisenhower issued a statement defending the U.S. position and promising to continue his efforts in pursuing world peace. He agreed to suspend further U.S. missions, but would not apologize for what he considered routine surveillance. Both Khrushchev's and Eisenhower's statements are excerpted below.

The summit, earlier planned by the two leaders with their counterparts—Britain's prime minister Harold Macmillan and France's president Charles de Gaulle—had aimed to discuss disarmament and ease global tensions, especially those between the United States and Russia. With neither the Soviet Union nor the United States willing to budge after making their respective statements, the summit collapsed and Khrushchev went home.

The failed summit was significant for two reasons. First, the hardline stance of the Soviets boosted Khrushchev's reputation and the credibility of the USSR. Second, Eisenhower's negotiating position was thought not to be tough enough, and many Americans believed he

Part I: Nikita Khrushchev, statement at the Paris Summit, May 16, 1960.
Part II: Dwight D. Eisenhower, statement at the Paris Summit, May 16, 1960.

was losing the Cold War. This paved the way for the election of John F. Kennedy to the presidency. Kennedy promised in his campaign to be more aggressive in dealing with communism.

Part I: Khrushchev's Statement

A provocative act is known to have been committed recently with regard to the Soviet Union by the American Air Force. It consisted in the fact that on May 1 a U.S. military reconnaissance aircraft invaded the Soviet Union while executing a specific espionage mission to obtain information on military and industrial installations on the territory of the USSR. After the aggressive purpose of its flight became known the aircraft was shot down by units of the Soviet rocket troops. Unfortunately, this was not the only case of aggressive and espionage actions by the U.S. Air Force against the Soviet Union. . . .

Now, at a time when the leaders of the governments of the four powers are arriving in Paris to take part in the conference, the question arises of how is it possible to productively negotiate and examine the questions confronting the conference when the U.S. government and the President himself have not only failed to condemn this provocative act—the intrusion of the American military aircraft into the Soviet Union—but, on the contrary, have declared that such actions will continue to be a state policy of the U.S.A. with regard to the Soviet Union. . . .

Soviets Threaten Action

The Soviet government reserves the right in all such cases to take the appropriate retaliatory measures against those who violate the state sovereignty of the USSR and engage in such espionage and sabotage regarding the Soviet Union. The USSR government reiterates that with regard to those states that by making their territory available for American military bases become accomplices in aggressive actions against the USSR, the appropriate measure will also be taken, not excluding a blow against these bases.

In this connection it is impossible to ignore the statement by President Eisenhower to the effect that under the threat of a peace treaty with the G.O.R. (East Germany) he could not take part in the summit conference, though what he called a threat was merely the declaration by the Soviet government of its firm resolve to do away with the vestiges of war in Europe and conclude a peace, and thus to bring the situation—particularly in West Berlin—in line with requirements of life and the interests of insuring the peace and security of the European nations. . . .

The U.S. Must Cease Provocations

If the U.S. government is really ready to co-operate with the governments of the other powers in the interests of maintaining peace and strengthening confidence between states it must, firstly, condemn the inadmissible provocative actions of the U.S. Air Force with regard to the Soviet Union and, secondly, from continuing such actions and such a policy against the USSR in the future. It goes without saying that in this case the U.S. government cannot fail to call to strict account those who are directly guilty of the deliberate violation by American aircraft of the state borders of the USSR.

Until this is done by the U.S. government the Soviet government sees no possibility for productive negotiations with the U.S. government at the summit conference. It cannot be among the participants in negotiations where one of them has made treachery the basis of his policy with regard to the Soviet Union. . . .

It stands to reason that if the U.S. government were to declare that in the future the United States will not violate the state borders of the USSR with its aircraft, that it deplores the provocative actions undertaken in the past, and will punish those directly guilty of such actions, which would assure the Soviet Union equal conditions with other powers, I as head of the Soviet government, would be ready to participate in the conference and exert all efforts to contribute to its success.

As a result of the provocative flights of American military aircraft and, above all, as a result of such provocative flights being declared the national policy of the United States of America for the future with regard to the Socialist countries, new conditions have appeared in international relationships. . . .

We therefore reject the conditions which the United States of America is creating for us. We cannot participate in any negotiations and in the solution of even those questions which have already matured. We cannot because we see that the United States has no desire to reach a settlement.

It is considered to be a leader in the western countries. Therefore the conference would at present be a useless waste of time and a deception of the public opinion of all countries. I repeat, we cannot under the obtaining situation take part in the negotiations.

We want to participate in the talks only on an equal footing, with equal opportunities for both one and the other side.

We consider it necessary for the people of all the countries of the world to understand us correctly. The Soviet Union is not renouncing efforts to achieve agreement. And we are sure that reasonable agreements are possible, but, evidently, not at this but at another time. . . .

We think that some time should be allowed to elapse so that the questions that have arisen should settle. . . .

We Believe in Peace

The Soviet Union on its part will not lessen its efforts to reach an agreement. I think that public opinion will correctly understand our position, will understand that we were deprived of the possibility to participate in these negotiations.

However, we firmly believe in the necessity of peaceful coexistence because to lose faith in peaceful coexistence would mean to doom mankind to war, would mean to agree with the inevitability of wars, and under the circumstances it is known what disasters would be brought by a war to all nations on our planet.

I wish to address the people of the United States of America. I was in the U.S.A. and met there with various sections of the American people and I am deeply convinced that all the strata of the American people do not want war. An exception constitutes but a small frantic group in the Pentagon and supporting it are militarist quarters which benefit from the armaments race, gaining huge profits, which disregard the interests of the American people and in general the interests of the peoples of all countries, and which pursue an adventurous policy.

We express gratitude to President de Gaulle for the hospitality and for rendering us the possibility to meet in Paris, the capital of France. We also appreciate the efforts of the government of Great Britain and of Prime Minister Macmillan personally.

We regret that this meeting has been torpedoed by the reactionary circles of the United States of America by provocative flights of American military planes over the Soviet Union.

We regret that this meeting has not brought about the results expected by all nations of the world.

Let the disgrace and responsibility for this rest with those who have proclaimed a bandit policy toward the Soviet Union.

As is known, President Eisenhower and I have agreed to exchange visits. Last September I made such a visit to the U.S.A. We were greatly gratified by that visit, the meetings and talks we had in the United States, and for all this we expressed our appreciation.

The President of the U.S.A. was to make a return visit to our country. Our agreement was that he would come to us on June 10. And we were being prepared to accord a good welcome to the high guest.

Eisenhower Calls Off Visit

Unfortunately, as a result of provocative and aggressive actions against the USSR there have been created now such conditions when we have been deprived of a possibility to receive the President with proper cordiality with which the Soviet people receive welcome guests. At present we cannot express such cordiality to the President of the U.S.A. since as the result of provocative flights of American military planes with reconnaissance purposes there are created conditions clearly unfavorable for this visit. The Soviet people cannot and do not want to be sly.

That is why we believe that at present the visit of the President of the U.S.A. to the Soviet Union should be postponed and agreement should be reached as to the time of the visit when the condition for the visit would mature. Then the Soviet people will be able to express proper cordiality and hospitality toward the high guest representing the great power with which we sincerely want to live in peace and friendship.

Part II: Eisenhower's Statement

I had previously been informed of the sense of the statement just read by Premier Khrushchev.

In my statement of May 11th and in the statement of Secretary [Christian] Herter of May 9th, the position of the United States was made clear with respect to the distasteful necessity of espionage activities in a world where nations distrust each other's intentions. We pointed out that these activities had no aggressive intent but rather were to assure the safety of the United States and the free world against surprise attack by a power which boasts of its ability to devastate the United States and other countries by missiles armed with atomic war heads. As is well known, not only the United States but most other countries are constantly the targets of elaborate and persistent espionage of the Soviet Union.

Flights Suspended

There is in the Soviet statement an evident misapprehension on one key point. It alleges that the United States has, through official statements, threatened continued overflights. The importance of this alleged threat was emphasized and repeated by Mr. Khrushchev. The United States has made no such threat. Neither I nor my government has intended any. The actual statements go no further than to say that the United States will not shirk its responsibility to safeguard against surprise attack.

In point of fact, these flights were suspended after the recent incident and are not to be resumed. Accordingly, this cannot be the issue.

I have come to Paris to seek agreements with the Soviet Union which would eliminate the necessity for all forms of espionage, including overflights. I see no reason to use this incident to disrupt the conference.

Proposal to the United Nations

Should it prove impossible, because of the Soviet attitude, to come to grips here in Paris with this problem and the other vital issues threatening world peace, I am planning in the near future to submit to the United Nations a proposal for the creation of a United Nations aerial surveillance to detect preparations for attack. This plan I had intended to place before this conference. This surveillance system would operate in the territories of all nations prepared to accept such inspection.

For its part, the United States is prepared not only to accept United Nations aerial surveillance but to do everything in its power to contribute to the rapid organization and successful operation of such international surveillance.

We of the United States are here to consider in good faith the important problems before this conference. We are prepared either to carry this point no further, or to undertake bilateral conversations between the United States and the USSR while the main conference proceeds.

Allied Support

My words were seconded and supported by my western colleagues, who also urged Mr. Khrushchev to pursue the path of reason and common sense and to forget propaganda. Such an attitude would have permitted the conference to proceed. Mr.

Khrushchev was left in no doubt by me that his ultimatum would never be acceptable to the United States.

Mr. Khrushchev brushed aside all arguments of reason and not only insisted upon this ultimatum, but also insisted that he was going to publish his statement in full at the time of his own choosing.

It was thus made apparent that he was determined to wreck the Paris conference.

In fact, the only conclusion that can be drawn from his behavior this morning was that he came all the way from Moscow to Paris with the sole intention of sabotaging this meeting on which so much of the hopes of the world have rested.

In spite of this serious and adverse development, I have no intention whatsoever to diminish my continuing efforts to promote progress toward a peace with justice. This applies to the remainder of my stay in Paris as well as thereafter.

New Missiles Are the Vanguard of America's Nuclear Deterrence

By Harold H. Martin

In July 1960 the U.S. Navy fired three Polaris missiles off the coast of Cape Canaveral, Florida. The Polaris was a new-generation solid-fueled rocket that could propel a warhead eleven hundred miles to a target. Harold H. Martin, editor at the *Saturday Evening Post*, writes in October 1960 that the Polaris, launched from a submerged submarine, can drop a thermonuclear warhead on any target in the world. He notes that the Polaris promises to be the United States's ultimate protection against nuclear attack by the Soviet Union.

Another innovative weapon that underwent testing in 1960 was the air force's Minuteman missile. The Minuteman was a land-based rocket fired from a concrete silo buried in the ground. Martin explains that the Minuteman's strength is its cost. It could be produced in great numbers to become the backbone of the United States's deterrent force. According to Martin, the military promises that swift, effective retaliation is assured if the Soviets ever launch a nuclear strike against the United States.

We know now that 1960 marks the beginning of a new era in the missile age. The gigantic liquid-fueled rockets, the Atlases and Titans, which have behaved—and misbehaved—so spectacularly in test firings at Canaveral, are first-generation weapons whose days were numbered from the start. The money we spent on them has not been wasted, for their development has taught us most of what we now know about missilery. Nor were they in any sense failures, for despite their ponderous complexity, we have developed in them a range and accuracy and a degree of dependability beyond anything we dreamed we could accomplish in 1954 when we entered belatedly into the missile race with the Soviets.

Soon, though, both the gigantic liquid-fueled missiles and the manned bomber will begin, in the airman's jargon, to "phase out." By 1965, under present plans, at least half of the swift bombers which now trace their vapor trails across the skies on their incessant training missions will have gone to the aerial boneyard—victims of a new technology. Their role as keepers of the peace will be taken over by a new family of weapons—the cheap-to-build, simple-to-operate, easy-to-move, handle, hide and protect, solid-fueled rockets that can stand armed, aimed and ready to fire at the flick of a switch.

The nuclear-weapon-carrying bomber, with all its electronics gear, is one of the most complicated pieces of machinery ever devised by man. The liquid-fueled rocket with its maze of pipes, valves, tanks and pumps is a plumber's nightmare. The engine of the solid-fueled rocket, on the other hand, is a simple casing of high-quality steel packed with a rubbery mass which looks like the stuff of which cheap gray pencil erasers are made. "It is," one Air Force officer said, "just a big garbage can loaded with a slow-burning bomb."

Retaliation Capability

The first member of this new family of solid-fueled weapons to become battle-ready will be the Navy's Polaris. As every reader knows by now, the nuclear-powered submarine *George Washington*, while submerged off Cape Canaveral last July, fired three Polaris missiles successfully. The bottle-shaped rocket popped from the depths on a blast of air, fired up its engine fifty feet above the surface, and propelled a simulated warhead 1100 miles to a downrange target. A fourth try failed, but the implication of the three successful shots must have been clear to Mr. Khrushchev: The Polaris works. Launched from submerged submarines lying off his coast, it can drop a thermonuclear warhead on nearly any of the Soviet's principal cities. It gives us a capacity not only for instantaneous but for inevitable retaliation. If the Soviets' capability to find and destroy a swift, silent, deep-running submarine is no greater than ours, the Polaris-carrying submarine, with its protective cordon of attack subs, is the most nearly invulnerable weapon we now possess.

The successful firing of the Polaris last July brought a lifting of the spirit to a country made nervous and jumpy by Mr. Khrushchev's ominous rumblings. Sometime this winter the Air Force will present its own spectacular entry in the new family of simple, solid-fuel weapons. From a concrete silo dug eighty-five feet into the sands of Cape Canaveral, a slim Air Force rocket called the Minuteman will rise in a gush of fire and smoke. If nothing goes amiss—and the half-dozen companies who are building the Minuteman are confident that nothing will—its simulated nuclear warhead will impact some twenty-odd minutes later on a target area 6300 miles downrange. Once it has been demonstrated that the missile can "blow and go" from its simple hole in the ground, it will be fired from a still basically simple platform—a railroad flatcar specially designed as a launching pad.

The Polaris holds out the promise that we can deploy missiles that are invulnerable to nuclear attack in all the waters that rim the Soviet world. The anticipated success of the silo Minuteman holds out the equally bright prospect that we can bury long-range weapons in hard sites which only a direct hit by a multimegaton warhead could destroy. The mobile Minuteman, riding on trains that wander over 80,000 miles of track would, the Air Force believes, be about as hard to target as a submarine. Any cowpuncher, sheep-herder or Soviet agent could see them parked briefly along a siding, poking skyward and ready to shoot, or moving to a new location at forty miles per hour. But to be sure of making a kill, the Soviets would have to blanket one third of the United States with high-yield missiles.

An Affordable Deterrent

The Minuteman will carry a less-powerful explosive than the huge Atlas or the gigantic Titan. Its range will be no greater than theirs and its guidance system, though smaller and lighter, will probably be no more accurate. The great breakthrough it achieves is not technological—although the development of the powerful solid fuels is a milestone in missilery—but economic. It is a missile we can afford to buy, not just in dozens or in hundreds, but in thousands, if need be. Man's war machines, from the stone-hurling catapult to the B-58 bomber, have grown progressively more complex and more costly. Minuteman, for the first time, reverses that trend. A squadron of fifty Minutemen buried in hard sites, aimed and ready to fire, according to Air Force figures, would cost about one fifth to one seventh as much as an equal number of Atlas or Titan missiles.

The Air Force, therefore, is naturally convinced that its simple, inexpensive, ever-ready Minuteman should be the backbone of our future deterrent force—at least until we can put a manned bomber into the upper atmosphere or a weapons-carrying satellite into orbit in outer space. The Navy is equally sure that the Polaris-carrying submarine, which costs some $120,000,000 with its weapons aboard, should assume the main deterrent role. The Navy now has fourteen in the works—finished, building or planned—and is asking for a total of forty-five, which would carry 720 missiles, each capable of destroying a city. . . .

By the summer of 1962, therefore, Minuteman should be ready, and the Strategic Air Command (SAC) will take it over as a fully operational weapon. The first three squadrons, totaling 150 missiles, will go into the ground in the vicinity of Malmstrom Air Base near Great Falls, Montana, and the Air Force is now busy acquiring land near other bases in the West.

Minuteman Sites

There will be nothing dramatic about a Minuteman site. Over an area of several hundred square miles will be scattered ten-foot-high wire fences, each enclosing some two acres of ground. In the center of each fenced area will be a twenty-ton concrete slab, set flush with the earth. Beneath this slab, with target information already cranked into its electronic brain, the missile will sit in its hole, sealed in a casing of plastic which will burn off as the missile is fired. Simple heating and cooling devices will keep the temperature in the hole within a range of 60 to 100 degrees, and humidity will be controlled. A few miles away, in a concrete capsule buried in the earth, two men will watch a control board. They are linked with a red telephone back at SAC's buried headquarters near Omaha, and by the pushing of a button, they can fire missiles in salvo if the coded word to shoot should come. Nobody will be near the missile itself. Sensing devices will flash a warning to the launch center if anything touches the fence, or if there is any movement within the fenced area or in the silo, and roving patrols will move by jeep or helicopter to investigate.

Though the missile can be launched in seconds, every precaution will be taken to prevent an inadvertent firing. No one man, out of boredom, drunkenness or insanity, can shoot. The order to fire must come from SAC, and the coded signal, changed every day, itself is needed to activate the weapon. Two or more launch centers must receive the coded order, or neither can fire. Thus, four men must agree that the order to fire is authentic. Even then, one man cannot shoot, for the two men in the launch center must perform certain simple acts simultaneously before the missile will fire.

A Counterforce

The Air Force has not yet announced how many Minutemen it thinks it will need. The number may run into the thousands, for the Air Force's concept is of a "counterforce," hardened or mobile enough to survive an initial attack and strong enough to retaliate against every military capability the Soviets may possess. The Navy view, as expressed by Adm. Arleigh Burke, Chief of Naval Operations, in a speech before the Chamber of Commerce in Charleston, South Carolina, is that "in general nuclear war, missile forces can no longer attempt to destroy their enemy's counterpart without destroying the corporate body of the enemy state itself. . . ." This means killing people, and people live in cities, and there is only a limited number of city targets. Therefore, the Navy holds, there is a limit to the retaliatory power we will need.

Around this divergence of opinion, other arguments will swirl as Congress holds hearings on the military budget. The Navy still believes that the nuclear aircraft carrier has a place in our arsenal—and the first one soon will be at sea. The Air Force believes as strongly that the manned B-70, flying at hypersonic speeds at the edge of the atmosphere, is essential to our safety. The Air Force also sees in the missile engine the vehicle which in time will launch manned reconnaissance satellites into space, or will put manned bombing platforms into orbit. The X-15 rocket plane and the Dyna-Soar are moves in these directions.

To prepare for that time when we do move into aerospace, when all of our old concepts of the separate roles and missions of the three services will have become obsolete, we should now reorganize the Department of Defense, the Air Force argues— beginning by putting all the strategic weapons, including SAC's bombers and missiles, and the Navy's Polaris, under one command. The idea has a certain appeal, for to put our warning system and our retaliatory power into outer space obviously would require the combined genius, valor and resources of all the services. The Navy, however, sees in this argument an Air Force effort to assume an ever-dominant role in our national defense.

Timothy Leary's First Psychedelic Gathering

By Bruce Cook

In his 1971 book, *The Beat Generation*, author Bruce Cook maintains that Harvard psychologist Timothy Leary played a pivotal role in propagating the psychedelic revolution that swept America and many parts of the world in the sixties. Cook traces Leary's initial drug-induced visionary experience to a trip in Mexico in August 1960 when he first tasted a mind-altering mushroom. It turned out that the so-called magic mushroom had been eaten by Indians for ages, long before Europeans set foot on the American continent in the fifteenth century. After discovering the magic mushroom, Timothy Leary set out to turn America on to psychedelic drugs. With the Center for Research in Personality at Harvard as his base, he started various projects that sought to discover the uses of the mushroom. He recruited students, faculty members, scholars, poets, and artists to join him in his experiments, the first of which took place at Leary's home in December 1960. Cook believes that Leary was the right man to change what he calls "the shape and substance" of life in America in the sixties.

O n a Saturday afternoon in August 1960, a thirty-nine-year-old member of the Harvard University psychology faculty sat with a group of friends and fellow researchers on the lawn of a rented villa in Cuernavaca, Mexico. In all, there were six men and women there, ranged in a circle around two large bowls of ugly black mushrooms. These were the so-called magic mushrooms that grow on the mountains around Mexico City. When eaten, they produce altered states of consciousness in the individual, a heightening and release of the senses, and ultimately visions as well. The Indians of the area have eaten them since long before the coming of the Spaniards; in defiance of the prohibitions of the Catholic Church they maintain a cult for the consumption of the sacred mushrooms.

None of those present that afternoon in Cuernavaca had ever before sampled the mushroom. The Harvard psychologist had taken no mind-changing drug stronger than alcohol, and so he quite naturally felt some trepidation when his turn came: "I picked one up. It stank of forest damp and crumbling logs and New England basement. Are you sure they are not poisonous?" Receiving some assurance, he put one into his mouth, then another and another, fighting back the nausea that swept over him in response to the foul, bitter taste of the mushrooms. But he washed them down with beer, and managed to swallow seven of them in all, without vomiting.

What happened then was four hours and seven minutes of an experience so unique and powerful that it not only changed the life of that psychologist, whose name of course was Timothy Leary, but it may ultimately also alter the shape and substance of life here in America. For from that "classic visionary voyage," Dr. Leary's first, followed the psychedelic revolution that swept America in the 1960s. Nothing has done quite so much to spread the fissure between generations as the passion of the younger one for drugs that alter or intensify consciousness. And no one has done quite so much to accelerate and propagate this passion as Timothy Leary. Whether or not the psychedelic revolution would have happened just as it did without him is open to doubt. The drugs were there certainly, and others—such as Aldous Huxley, Gerald Heard, and Alan Watts—were working to get them better known. But Dr. Leary had so many qualities that made him just the right man for the moment. He was, among other things, a respected research psychologist and a man unafraid to break the rules and buck the establishment; he was an apostate Catholic who through most of his life nursed an unsatisfied desire to play the role of messiah; he was, in his own way, quite modest, yet willing to do almost anything to publicize his cause and win converts to it; he was utterly sincere and at the same time a bit of a charlatan.

Early Experiments

In the beginning, not even Dr. Timothy Leary knew all this about himself. At the time he sat down in Cuernavaca to eat those mushrooms in fact, there were a good many things he did not know. He knew nothing of Aldous Huxley's experiment with the drug mescaline (synthetic peyote) described so vividly in *The Doors of Perception*. He had not heard about the synthesis of the spectacular mind-expander, lysergic acid diethylamide [LSD], by the Swiss research chemist Dr. Albert Hoffman. And when he went so far as to describe his visionary experience to another psychologist, he was told that it all sounded very much like marijuana. But Dr. Leary didn't know, for though he had often heard of the stuff being smoked by Beats in San Francisco and Greenwich Village, he had never actually tried it himself. He then reflected: "This was some development! Was that all I had experienced? Were the mystic visions and the oriental dreams just a stronger version of a Greenwich Village pot high? I had been sure we were on the verge of something new and great. A pushing back of the frontiers of consciousness. But now it looked as though I was just a naive, sheltered intellectual discovering what hip teen-agers on the North Beach [in San Francisco] had been experiencing for years."

But no North Beach teen-ager could have proselytized for marijuana as he did for the mushroom. As soon as he got back to Harvard, he and his coworker there, Richard Alpert (who was also present that afternoon in Cuernavaca), got to work on projects to legitimate the taking of the drug. They wanted to find out what it could do. They wanted to discover what its uses might be as a tool in clinical psychology. Thus the Center for Research in Personality was founded, and from it came a number of interesting projects, the most successful of which was a group counseling program at the Massachusetts State Prison in Concord in which inmates were given psilocybin on a regular basis to break down psychological patterns that confirmed them in recidivism.

The Center gave Dr. Leary a base of operations from which he planned the strategy for his campaign to turn America on to visionary drugs. He thought of it, truly enough, as a religious crusade, and no zealot ever went after converts with a more intense missionary zeal. Faculty members, graduate students, anyone in fact who seemed mature enough to handle such a powerful drug was given the chance to do so by Timothy Leary.

He was especially avid to attract writers and intellectuals who had—or might be persuaded to have—some interest in this area. Arthur Koestler, for instance, was known even then for his investigations into the physiology of thought and consciousness, and he had just published a book called *The Lotus and the Robot*, in which he had dismissed the mysticism of the East as having virtually no worth to modern man. Leary wanted to see him on both counts—to discuss his investigations and to send him on a psilocybin trip that might change his mind regarding the Orient. And so he wrote Koestler a letter so full of boyish enthusiasm that it must have made even the dour Hungarian smile. Leary concluded, urging him to give the mushrooms a try: "We are offering the experience to distinguished creative people. Artists, poets, writers, scholars. We've learned a tremendous amount by listening to them. . . ." Eventually Koestler did show up, had a disastrous paranoiac experience, and left even more hostile to drugs and visions than he had come. "This pressure-cooker mysticism seemed the ultimate profanation," he later commented.

Fellow Voyagers

But Koestler was only one of many who came by. Among those "distinguished creative people" mentioned by Leary were Charles Olson, William S. Burroughs, and of course, Allen Ginsberg. Ginsberg rates an "of course" here because Timothy Leary himself has given an enormous amount of credit to the poet for the part he played in furthering the work. He is so generous in his praise ("Allen taught us courage—taught us not to be afraid in facing those unknown realms of consciousness which are opened by psychedelic drugs") that Allen Ginsberg is thought by some to have played a much more active role in the psychedelic revolution than, in fact, he did. But from the beginning, apparently, Ginsberg and Leary have felt quite close. And the reasons for this seem to stem directly from that first psychedelic summit which took place at Leary's home in Cambridge.

Allen Ginsberg, of course, was no newcomer to the drug scene. As early as his Columbia years in New York, he had become well acquainted with the narcotics milieu through Burroughs and Herbert Huncke. In San Francisco he had smoked marijuana and

Timothy Leary encouraged people to seek spiritual enlightenment through the use of psychedelic drugs.

taken drugs of the amphetamine variety. And he had heard— again, from Burroughs—of the effects of various mind-opening drugs encountered on expedition through parts of South America.

At the time Dr. Leary invited him up to Harvard for his session in December 1960, Allen Ginsberg had recently followed Burroughs's trail to the Peruvian jungles and had had some experience with the psychedelic drugs, mescaline and LSD-25— all documented and dutifully recorded in poems from the period. As with all the early Leary sessions, however, this one was to involve the taking of the synthetic mushroom drug, psilocybin. In fact, Timothy Leary did not himself take LSD, the drug with which he became so closely identified, until just about a year later. He welcomed Ginsberg as a visiting guru and interrogated him closely on matters of primitive belief and ritual practice among Indians that involved the taking of drugs. The poet regaled him with bits of narcotic lore learned from Burroughs, and he told him what he himself had seen, heard, and experienced in New York, Berkeley, and Morocco.

As for the session itself, there is a long and complete account of it in Leary's book, *High Priest.* It reads like a chapter in the great comic psychedelic novel that he may, after all someday come to write—we see Ginsberg capering naked through the halls of Leary's home, then running to the telephone to call Jack Kerouac and tell him all about this great experience he is having. The action ends in the kitchen. Ginsberg, now back to earth, puts his mind to what he can do to promote the psychedelic experience to the media. He goes through the address book he always carries with him and considers his list of friends and contacts, promising to turn them all on. Leary was delighted. He concluded that shouting it from the housetops the way this "Zen master politician" urged him to might, after all, be the best course: "Allen Ginsberg came to Harvard and shook us loose from our academic fears and strengthened our courage and faith in the process."

Regarding the visit of William S. Burroughs, Timothy Leary was somewhat more equivocal. Burroughs seems to have scared him just a little—or, in any case, left him feeling a little less certain of his mission. Ginsberg had urged him to invite Burroughs for a session: "He knows more about drugs than anyone alive. What a report he'll write for you!" Leary sent him some psilocybin pills; he heard in a short time that Burroughs had had a bad trip on DMT, a related drug, and wasn't much interested in the pills from Harvard. He and Leary met on a couple of occasions in Morocco and London, sparred tentatively without decision, and finally got together at Harvard in the summer of 1961. Burroughs had then only recently kicked heroin with the help of apomorphine, and with one bad psychedelic trip on DMT behind him, he was understandably less than sanguine about this grand new experience that Leary was urging upon him. Although he got him to *smoke* a little of the magic mushroom that had been dried and sent up from Oaxaca, and Burroughs conceded along the way that he was feeling a little high, Leary never really broke down his resistance. He left the Harvard researchers high and dry. And the impression was clear that they had failed to measure up to some high standard that, though never articulated, was carefully maintained. They had to accept that. William S. Burroughs is a man to whom it is very difficult indeed to feel superior.

A Ticket to Direct Religious Experience

It may seem to some that in emphasizing the link between Leary and the Beats I am doing a disservice to them. For he did, it is true, go to rather giddy extremes in promoting drug-taking as a cult, coming on, as he did, as a kind of pill priest whose half-baked religious ideas and vocabulary were borrowed from the Roman Catholicism into which he had been born. He became so enthusiastic about psychedelics—LSD, in particular—that he began recommending them almost indiscriminately, refusing to concede even the possibility of ill effects. And if he was railroaded on that marijuana charge (thirty years for a stash discovered on his daughter's person), nevertheless, he seemed by then almost to have sought imprisonment as martyrdom.

There are a couple of things, however, that should be said in Timothy Leary's behalf. First, and most obvious, he is sincere. He believes quite honestly in the general efficacy of the psychedelic drugs; he is certain that their real importance to man is as a means to direct religious experience; and he is also probably convinced personally that reports of recurring psychosis and genetic damage from LSD have been greatly exaggerated.

There is also this: While Leary has always laid doubtful claim to the future as being on his side (after all, only time will tell), he and all the little Robespierres of the drug revolution can make more certain claim to the past. Drug-taking of one kind or another has been with us so long in so many different cultures and forms as to make it seem universal. The practice springs, in the view of Aldous Huxley, from something deep in man's very nature.

The Birth of SNCC Unveils a New Generation of Black Activism

By Clayborne Carson

The Student Nonviolent Coordinating Committee (SNCC), founded in April 1960 in Raleigh, North Carolina, transformed the ad hoc groups of students who had organized scattered civil rights demonstrations after the Greensboro sit-in into a broad and sustained student movement that would press for a wider program of social reform. In an excerpt from his 1981 history of SNCC (pronounced "snick"), history professor Clayborne Carson asserts that the new group not only confirmed its commitment to nonviolence but also sought to maintain its independence from the older civil rights organizations and develop new leadership among its ranks. They vowed to share experiences gained in recent protests and to chart future goals. Carson traces SNCC's philosophy to the guiding principles laid out by Ella Baker, an experienced student activist who had worked with Martin Luther King Jr.'s Southern Christian Leadership Conference (SCLC).

Clayborne Carson, who is on the faculty of Stanford University, has written extensively on African American and civil rights history. He is the author of *In Struggle: SNCC and the Black Awakening of the 1960s* and *Malcolm X: The FBI File*. He is also the editor of *The Autobiography of Martin Luther King Jr.*, coeditor of *Eyes on the Prize: America's*

Civil Rights Years, and the senior editor of the three-volume *The Papers of Martin Luther King Jr.*

SNCC was born during a period of extensive student protest activity. Yet its creation indicated the culmination of the lunch counter sit-in movement rather than the beginning of a new upsurge of student activism. SNCC exerted little control over the ad hoc protest groups throughout the South whose activities it was supposed to coordinate. Only as the spontaneous enthusiasm of the early protests waned did the new organization begin to attract support.

SNCC's founding conference, held on April 16–18, 1960, in Raleigh, North Carolina, was called by Ella Baker, executive director of SCLC. The initiating role of SCLC might have signaled the reassertion of control over the southern black struggle by Martin Luther King and the black ministers associated with him, but Baker, who understood the psychological need of student activists to remain independent of adult control, resisted efforts to subvert their autonomy. Students at the conference affirmed their commitment to the nonviolent doctrines popularized by King, yet they were drawn to these ideas not because of King's advocacy but because they provided an appropriate rationale for student protest.

SNCC's founding was an important step in the transformation of a limited student movement to desegregate lunch counters into a broad and sustained movement to achieve major social reforms. Although many of the students at the founding conference initially were reluctant to broaden the focus of their activities, the existence of a South-wide coordinating committee provided the opportunity for increasing numbers of young people to participate in a regional movement that would attack racism in all its dimensions.

The Raleigh Conference

Baker initiated the plan to bring sit-in protesters together at Raleigh because she recognized that many black students had little preparation for the leadership roles suddenly thrust upon them. As a product of a southern black college, Shaw University in Raleigh, she was herself aware of the limitations of southern black education and of the significance of the sit-ins as a departure from the pattern of political apathy among black students. She hoped that a meeting of student leaders would enable protesters to communicate with each other and to acquire the knowledge necessary to sustain their movement. After borrowing $800 from SCLC and contacting an acquaintance at Shaw to secure facilities there, she sent a note, signed by herself and King, to all major protest groups, asking them to send representatives.

Baker carefully avoided any implication that the meeting would subvert the independence of local student protest groups. Rather, student leaders were offered the opportunity "TO SHARE experience gained in recent protest demonstrations and TO HELP chart future goals for effective action." The notice lauded the leadership already shown by black students and called for "evaluation in terms of where do we go from here." The purpose of the meeting was to achieve "a more unified sense of direction for *training and action in Nonviolent Resistance.*" The letter assured students that, although "Adult Freedom Fighters" would be present "for counsel and guidance," the conference would be "youth centered."

Although Baker's invitation did not suggest that the Raleigh conference would result in the formation of a lasting organization, her long career as a social reformer had convinced her of the need for a new type of protest group to stimulate mass struggle among blacks. Born in Virginia in 1905 and raised in North Carolina, Baker had hoped to become a medical missionary, but upon finding that the cost of medical training exceeded her family's means, she turned to sociology. After graduating as valedictorian of her college class, Baker went to New York and during the Depression worked as a community organizer while taking graduate courses at the New School for Social Research. During the 1940s she became a field secretary for the National Association for the Advancement of Colored People (NAACP) in New York. In January 1958 she made what was meant to be a short trip to Atlanta to help organize a series of mass meetings for the newly established SCLC; instead, she remained to organize SCLC's headquarters. Soon, however, she became restive under the cautious leadership of King and was planning to resign her post when the lunch counter sit-ins began.

During the spring of 1960, Baker commended the "inclination toward group-centered leadership" among the students. Undoubtedly referring to her experiences with King, she noted that such a trend was "refreshing" to those who bore "the scars of battle, the frustration and the disillusionment that come when the prophetic leader turns out to have heavy feet of clay." What was needed in a social movement, she later commented, was "the development of people who are interested not in being leaders as much as in developing leadership among other people."

The conference called by Baker was the most successful of several gatherings of sit-in leaders to take place during the spring. It attracted more than 120 black student activists representing 56 colleges and high schools in twelve southern states and the District of Columbia. Also attending were observers from thirteen student and social reform organizations, representatives from northern and border state colleges, and a dozen southern white students. In addition to the SCLC, the organizations taking part included Congress of Racial Equality (CORE) and the Fellowship of Reconciliation (FOR), both of which had long been engaged in the use of nonviolent direct action to achieve social reform. Among the student organizations represented were the National Student Association (NSA), Students for a Democratic Society (SDS), and National Student Christian Federation.

One of the largest delegations at the Raleigh conference, and the one that would subsequently provide SNCC with a disproportionate share of its leaders, was the Nashville student group. Though coming from varied backgrounds, the Nashville activists shared a commitment not simply to desegregation but also to Gandhiism and to the Christian ideal of "the beloved community." Fisk University provided a number of these protest leaders, most notably Marion Barry and Diane Nash. . . .

The most influential of the Nashville leaders was James Lawson, who grew up in the North and attended Baldwin-Wallace College in Ohio. Expelled from the Vanderbilt School of Theology for his involvement in sit-in protests, Lawson was, of all those attending the Raleigh meeting, the most familiar with the philosophical doctrines associated with nonviolent direct action. In the early 1950s he had chosen to go to prison rather than serve in the military during the Korean War. After being paroled to the Methodist Board of Missions, he spent three years as a missionary in India, where he studied Mahatma Gandhi's use of nonviolence to achieve political change. Lawson then attended the Oberlin College School of Theology and became the first southern field secretary of FOR.

On one of his trips through the South, Lawson, along with another FOR representative, Glenn Smiley, organized a workshop on nonviolence for the Nashville Christian Leadership Council, which was held in March 1958. After enrolling as a theology student, Lawson opened a similar workshop at Vanderbilt University in Nashville in early 1959. The workshop attracted a small group of black students, including Nash, Barry, [John] Lewis, and [James] Bevel, who were interested in using nonviolent tactics to achieve desegregation in downtown dining facilities. During the fall of 1959, they staged test sit-ins in an unsuccessful attempt to prod Nashville businessmen to desegregate voluntarily. When in February 1960 Lawson received news of the sit-in in Greensboro, the Nashville students were prepared to lead one of the most disciplined and sustained of the early protests. More than 150 students, including Lawson, were arrested in Nashville during the spring before the city leaders finally agreed to desegregate some lunch counters.

The Nashville students maintained firm control over the protests, ensuring that they remained nonviolent. Their rules of conduct for demonstrators became a model for protest movements elsewhere in the South. Among other items, they specified: "Don't strike back or curse if abused. . . . Show yourself courteous and friendly at all times. . . . Report all serious incidents to your leader in a polite manner. Remember love and nonviolence."

A Philosophy of Nonviolence

When the Raleigh conference opened, King, then thirty-one years old, was the center of attention. Indeed, his presence probably contributed to the large attendance. At a press conference before the opening session, King laid out an agenda for the students that presaged later trends within the southern struggle. In addition to suggesting a nationwide campaign of "selective buying," King advised the students to establish a permanent organization, collect a group of volunteers willing to go to jail rather than pay fines, and take the "freedom struggle" into all parts of the South to compel the intervention of the federal government. He also urged the students to learn more about the philosophy of nonviolence.

Although King outlined much of the future strategy of the student movement, he had less impact on the students than did Lawson, who was then little known outside Nashville. Lawson expressed a visionary set of ideas that distinguished the student activists both from the rest of society and from more moderate civil rights leaders. He insisted that the basic issues behind the protest were neither legal, sociological, nor radical, but moral and spiritual. The nonviolent protests had forced white southerners to recognize the existence of sin. Its "radically Christian methods" had stripped the "segregationist power structure of its major weapon: the manipulation of law or law-enforcement to keep the Negro in his place." In addition, the nonviolent movement was an attempt to speed the pace of social change. "All of Africa," Lawson warned, "will be free before the American Negro attains first class citizenship. Most of us will be grandparents before we can live normal human lives." In his most controversial statement, Lawson called the sit-in tactic "a judgment upon middle-class conventional, half-way efforts to deal with radical social evil." He specifically criticized the NAACP for emphasizing "fund-raising and court action rather than developing our greatest resource, a people no longer the victims of racial evil who can act in a disciplined manner to implement the constitution."

Lawson's influence was evident in the conference's general emphasis on nonviolence. When one delegate suggested that a decision be reached on the "goals, philosophy, future, and structure of the movement," Lawson insisted that the first two items be reversed and that the delegates first discuss the philosophy of nonviolence and then the goal of integration. Although there was resistance on the part of some students who were more concerned with action than philosophy, Lawson secured adoption of his statement of purpose which expressed the religious underpinnings of nonviolent direct action:

> We affirm the philosophical or religious ideal of nonviolence as the foundation of our purpose, the presupposition of our faith, and the manner of our action. Nonviolence as it grows from Judaic-Christian traditions seeks a social order of justice permeated by love. Integration of human endeavor represents the crucial first step towards such a society.

> Through nonviolence, courage displaces fear; love transforms hate. Acceptance dissipates prejudice; hope ends despair. Peace dominates war; faith reconciles doubt. Mutual regard cancels enmity. Justice for all overthrows injustice. The redemptive community supersedes systems of gross social immorality. . . .

Students in Charge

Baker recalled that forces were at work "to try to attach the young people to on-going organizations," but she thought "they had the right to direct their own affairs and even make their own mistakes." She knew from experience "how people and their ideas can be captured by those who have programs of their own." The students were willing to meet "on the basis of equality, but were intolerant of anything that smacked of manipulation or domination." Baker's views coincided with those of the black students. "She was much older in terms of age," recalled Lewis, "but I think in terms of ideas and philosophy and commitment she was one of the youngest persons in the movement."

With Baker's encouragement, the students voted to establish a temporary Student Nonviolent Coordinating Committee. It would have no official ties but would cooperate with all civil rights organizations. SNCC was established on the understanding that its permanent status would be determined at a future meeting of students. . . .

The Raleigh conference represented the peak of influence within SNCC for Lawson and his Nashville group. Determined to finish his theological studies, Lawson enrolled later in the spring of 1960 at Boston University, where that summer he received a Bachelor of Sacred Theology degree. . . . As the influence of the Lawson group waned, secular influences grew in importance. Nonetheless, the rhetoric of nonviolent direct action and the moralistic orientation of the Nashville movement continued to pervade SNCC through the early 1960s.

On May 13 and 14 eleven students met in Atlanta for the first official meeting of SNCC. Although it still had no operating funds or even an office, the students apparently expected to attract support, because they voted to hire a temporary office worker to sustain the organization during the summer. The establishment of a functioning organization was made possible when Baker offered SNCC a corner of the SCLC headquarters in Atlanta for use as an office and made available to the students SCLC's mailing facilities. Baker also recruited Jane Stembridge, daughter of a white Baptist minister from Virginia and a student at Union Theological Seminary, to run the SNCC office until a permanent administrative secretary could be found. . . .

Although by the summer of 1960 a few black students saw SNCC as an important, independent voice for the protest movement, the survival of the new group was by no means assured. Other student and civil rights organizations encouraged SNCC's emergence as a permanent organization, since it offered them a

central point of contact with southern black activists. The director of NSA's southern programs, Constance Curry, was particularly helpful in SNCC's early months, offering the use of NSA
equipment and facilities in Atlanta at a time when SNCC had few
resources of its own. Despite such backing, SNCC would probably not have survived its first summer had it not been for the en-
ergy and skills of Baker and Stembridge. Whereas SNCC appeared to outsiders and even to many black student leaders to be
merely a clearinghouse for the exchange of information about
localized protest movements, to the two women it was potentially
an organization for expanding the struggle beyond its campus
base to include all classes of blacks.

In July Baker and Stembridge were joined by Robert Moses,
a former graduate student at Harvard University. Moses . . . went
to Atlanta to work on an SCLC voter registration project. . . .

Voter Registration in Mississippi

He soon discovered that he and Stembridge had a common interest in Christian theology and mysticism and shared a skepti-
cism regarding King's leadership. When Stembridge suggested
that Moses assist SNCC by recruiting black leaders in the deep
South for an October conference, he eagerly agreed. . . .

The decision proved fateful both for Moses and for SNCC. At
Baker's suggestion, he met with Amzie Moore, head of the
NAACP chapter in Cleveland, Mississippi. Moore was one of a
small group of people who had kept the civil rights struggle in
the deep South alive despite violence and intimidation. When
Moses invited Moore to attend the SNCC conference, Moore accepted but made clear that his main concern was voter registration rather than desegregation. He suggested that SNCC send students to Mississippi to assist in a voter registration drive that
could ultimately result in the overthrow of the segregationist
regime in that state. Impressed by Moore's vision and determi-
nation, Moses promised he would return to take part in the Mississippi effort. Although Moses was not yet even a member of
SNCC's staff, this short meeting signaled the beginning of a
black struggle in Mississippi that would decisively shape
SNCC's future development.

Apart from Moses' trip to the deep South, the most significant
of SNCC's activities during the summer occurred at the Democratic and Republican conventions. Barry and other SNCC rep-

resentatives were given an opportunity to address members of the platform committees of each party, and their statements revealed the increasing concern of black student leaders with issues beyond desegregation. At the Democratic convention, for example, SNCC representatives proposed that delegates and candidates "stop playing political football with the civil rights of eighteen million Negro Americans" and take immediate action to desegregate public schools, expand job opportunities for blacks in the federal government and with federal contractors, grant self-government for the District of Columbia, and increase federal protection for blacks seeking to vote or exercise their civil rights. . . .

An Organizational Structure

At a fall conference in Atlanta on October 14–16, 1960, SNCC attempted to consolidate the student protest movement by establishing an organizational structure and clarifying its goals and principles. The invitation to the conference stressed that it would be "action-oriented" because SNCC leaders were "convinced that truth comes from being involved and not from observation and speculation. We are further convinced that only mass action is strong enough to force all of America to assume responsibility and that nonviolent direct action alone is strong enough to enable all of America to understand the responsibility she must assume.". . . .

About 140 delegates, alternatives, and observers from 46 protest centers attended the conference, as well as over 80 observers from northern colleges and sympathetic organizations. Unlike the Raleigh conference, which occurred during a period of extensive protest activity, the conference in Atlanta attracted only the hard core of students who remained involved in the movement after the initial level of black student activism declined. These southern student leaders came together with representatives of student and social reform organizations throughout the country who wanted to establish ties with the southern protest movement. A significant aspect of the conference was the presence of representatives from groups advocating Marxist ideas and interracial coalitions. Among the leftist groups represented were the Socialist party and its youth wing, the Young People's Socialist League, the newly formed SDS, the Southern Conference Educational Fund (SCEF), and the Highlander Folk School, a training school for labor organizers. . . .

The principal accomplishment of the conference was to create a permanent organizational structure for SNCC. The delegates established a Coordinating Committee to be composed of one representative from each southern state and the District of Columbia. Delegates nevertheless remained reluctant to give the reorganized SNCC much power. Local protest groups were allowed to remain autonomous, and all members of the committee could speak for the movement. . . .

The only action proposal considered by the delegates was one backed by socialist representatives to stage demonstrations on election day demanding that presidential candidates John Kennedy and Richard Nixon take positive stands on civil rights issues. Although the proposal was adopted and a few election day protests were conducted, a demonstration engineered by Atlanta student activists at the end of the conference had a much greater impact on the election. By convincing King to be arrested with them in a protest against discriminatory policies at Rich's department store in Atlanta, the students put national political leaders on the spot. Highly publicized telephone calls expressing concern from John Kennedy to King's wife and from Robert Kennedy to the judge handling the case undoubtedly increased John Kennedy's black support and contributed to his narrow victory over Nixon, who chose not to involve himself.

Although socialists had some influence at the conference, most black students did not accept even moderately socialist ideas. Bayard Rustin, a leader of the League for Industrial Democracy and King's adviser, was first invited to address the conference and then the invitation was withdrawn when a union sponsoring the conference objected to Rustin's radical reputation. The decision to rescind the invitation, however, was the only significant instance in which SNCC leaders capitulated to such pressures. Julian Bond later commented that the barring of Rustin gave the students "their first lesson in the proper exercise of civil liberties." Interestingly, a few years later SNCC leaders would clash with Rustin because they considered him too moderate and entrenched in the liberal establishment.

A Broader Agenda

The October conference marked a turning point in the development of the student protest movement. SNCC gained permanent status, and its student leaders became increasingly confident of their ability to formulate the future course of the movement. The conference also revealed a general trend in the protest movement toward a greater emphasis on political issues rather than on the religious ideals expressed by Lawson. . . .

Another indication of the broadening of student concerns was the visit of Edward King, SNCC's new administrative secretary, to Fayette County, Tennessee, to offer support to black tenants who had been evicted from farms for registering to vote. SNCC also supported the proposal of its affiliate, the Nonviolent Action Group (NAG) at Howard University, that the President and Congress aid blacks in Tennessee and cancel government contracts with firms which discriminated against blacks who attempted to vote. SNCC later requested that Fayette and Haywood counties be placed on the State Department's roster for technical assistance from the newly organized Peace Corps.

Even as SNCC leaders began to involve themselves in activities other than the desegregation of public facilities, they still had not resolved the issue of whether SNCC should be primarily a medium of communication and coordination among protest groups or an initiator of protest activities and civil rights projects. Baker's notion of "group-centered leadership" had taken hold among student activists, and they strongly opposed any hierarchy of authority such as existed in other civil rights organizations. The guidelines adopted at the November meeting limited SNCC to a "suggestive rather than directive" role in relation to local protest groups. . . .

The reluctance of the Coordinating Committee to assume a more assertive role resulted from the belief of most student activists that local autonomy was the basis of sustained militancy. Throughout its history SNCC would continue to support the notion that local community groups should determine their own direction. But the lull in protest activity since the spring of 1960 led some students by the end of the year to suspect that they, as representatives of SNCC, must take action to restore the movement. Only when SNCC workers were prepared to initiate protests outside their own communities could they begin to revive and extend the social struggle that had already become a central focus of their lives.

Malcolm X and Bayard Rustin Debate Approaches to the Race Issue

By Malcolm X and Bayard Rustin

In the following debate transcript, two black leaders present opposing visions on the creation of a society in the United States that is not plagued by racial antagonism. The young and charismatic Malcolm X draws from the separatist teachings of the Nation of Islam, a black church that is as much a political action association as it is a religious institution. He argues that the "Negro problem" can be solved through a moral reformation among blacks and the creation of a separate state, either in America or elsewhere, where blacks can have the full freedom and citizenship that have been denied them for centuries.

To this separatist view, Bayard Rustin—a key figure of the civil rights movement defined by the integrationist philosophies of A. Philip Randolph and Dr. Martin Luther King Jr.—offers an alternative. Rustin asserts that the integration of blacks into American society is possible and can be done through peaceful, nonviolent means.

Both men presented their views in a radio debate that took place in New York in November 1960. A host moderator posed questions that elicited the highly reasoned discussion that is presented below. Malcolm X's persuasive rhetoric generated a mass following for the Nation

Malcolm X and Bayard Rustin, WRAI radio debate, November 1960. Copyright © 1960 by the Bayard Rustin Fund. Reproduced by permission.

of Islam whose membership grew from five hundred in 1952 to thirty
thousand in 1963. Malcolm left the Nation of Islam after a falling out
with Elijah Muhammad, the organization's leader. He was assassinated
in 1965 while speaking to an audience in Manhattan. Rustin, who
played a major role in the civil rights movement, had a lifelong career
in social and political activism. A pacifist and a democratic socialist, he
was associated with the Fellowship of Reconciliation, the Congress of
Racial Equality, the A. Randolph Institute, and several other organizations committed to democracy, peace, and justice. He died in 1987.

Host: Tell us about your organization and what it stands
for.
Malcolm X: In the past two years, the Honorable
Elijah Muhammad has become the most talked about black man
in America because he is having such miraculous success in getting his program over among the so-called Negro masses. *Time*
magazine last year [1959] wrote that he has eliminated from
among his followers alcohol, dope addiction, profanity—all of
which stems from disrespect of self. He has successfully eliminated stealing and crime among his followers. *Time* also pointed
out that he has eliminated adultery and fornication, and prosti-
tution, making black men respect their women, something that
has been characteristically absent among our men. *Time* also
pointed out that Muslims, followers of Elijah Muhammad, have
eliminated juvenile delinquency.

When you think about it, *Time* was giving Mr. Muhammad
credit for being one of the greatest moral reformers that has appeared among the so-called Negroes yet. A few months later,
U.S. News & World Report pointed out that Mr. Muhammad was
successful in stressing the importance of economics. The point
behind his program, farms to feed our people, factories to manufacture goods for ourselves, businesses to create jobs for ourselves, is to be economically independent rather than sit around
waiting for the white man to give us jobs.

What the Honorable Elijah Muhammad has been teaching is
not what we have been accused of: nationalism. Nationalism is
the political approach to the problems that are confronting the
so-called Negro in America. The aim of the black nationalist is
the same as the aim of the Muslim. We are pointing toward the
same goal. But the difference is in method. We say the only so-

lution is the religious approach; this is why we stress the importance of a moral reformation. I would like to stress that Mr. Muhammad is not a politician. He does not believe politics is the solution to the so-called Negro's problem. It will take God. God will have to have a hand in it, because the problem of the so-called Negro is different from the problems of any other black people anywhere on this earth since the beginning of time. Every condition of the so-called Negro was pre-ordained and prophesied. And we believe that we are living in the fulfillment of that prophecy today. We believe that our history in America, our experiences at the hands of slave masters, is in line with Biblical prophecy. And we believe that Mr. Muhammad's presence among so-called Negroes here in America is in line with Biblical prophecies.

Host: Does this involve the creation of a separate state in America?

Malcolm X: It involves the creation of a black state for the black man if not in America then somewhere on this earth. If not abroad, then here in America. Primarily it involves acquiring some land that the black man can call his own. If the powers that be don't want it here, then they should make it possible for us to do it somewhere else.

Host: It does involve politics, then.

Malcolm X: Any religion that does not take into consideration the freedom and the rights of the black man is the wrong religion. But politics as such is not the solution. But the divine solution would have to have that ingredient in it. You can call it politics if you want, but the overall problem of the so-called Negro in America is not a political problem as such, it is an economic problem, a social problem, a mental problem, and a spiritual problem. Only God can solve the whole problem.

The Inevitability of Separatism?

Rustin: I am very happy to be here and I think Malcolm X can clarify some of the questions he has brought up in my mind. I believe the great majority of the Negro people, black people, are not seeking anything from anyone. They are seeking to become full-fledged citizens. Their ancestors have toiled in this country, contributing greatly to it. The United States belongs to no particular people, and in my view the great majority of Negroes and their leaders take integration as their key word—which means that rightly or wrongly they seek to become an integral part of the United States. We have, I believe, much work yet to do, both politically and through the courts, but I believe we have reached the point where most Negroes, from a sense of dignity and pride, have organized themselves to demand to become an integral part of all the institutions of the U.S. We are doing things by direct action which we feel will further this cause. We believe that justice for all people, including Negroes, can be achieved.

This is not a unique position, and while a controversial one it is certainly not as controversial as the one Malcolm X supports. Therefore I would like to ask him this question: The logic of your position is to say to black people in this country: "We have to migrate and set up some state in Africa." It seems to me that this is where you have to come out.

Malcolm X: Well, Mr. Rustin, let me say this about "full-fledged" or as they say "first-class" citizenship. Most of the so-called Negro leaders have got the Negro masses used to thinking in terms of second-class citizenship, of which there is no such

Malcolm X believed that blacks would obtain first-class citizenship only through moral reformation and the creation of a separate state.

thing. We who follow the Honorable Elijah Muhammad believe that a man is either a citizen or he is not a citizen. He is not a citizen by degree. If the black man in America is not recognized as a first-class citizen, we don't feel that he is a citizen at all. People come here from Hungary and are integrated into the American way of life overnight, they are not put into any fourth class or third class or any kind of class. The only one who is put in this category is the so-called Negro who is forced to beg the white man to accept him. We feel that if 100 years after the so-called Emancipation Proclamation the black man is still not free, then we don't feel that what Lincoln did set them free in the first place.

Rustin: This is all well and good but you are not answering my question.

Malcolm X: I am answering your question. The black man in America, once he gets his so-called freedom is still 9,000 miles away from that which he can call home. His problem is different from that of others who are striving for freedom. In other countries they are the majority and the oppressor is the minority. But here, the oppressor is the majority. The white man can just let you sit down. He can find someone else to run his factories.

So we don't think the passive approach can work here. And we don't see that anyone other than the so-called Negro was encouraged to seek freedom this way. The liberals tell the so-called Negro to use the passive approach and turn the other cheek, but they have never told whites who were in bondage to use the passive approach. They don't tell the whites in Eastern Europe who are under the Russian yoke to be passive in their resistance. They give them guns and make heroes out of them and call them freedom fighters. But if a black man becomes militant in his striving against oppression then immediately he is classified as a fanatic.

The white man is posing as the leader of the so-called Free World, and the only way he can be accepted as the leader of the so-called Free World is to be accepted by the majority of the people on this earth, the majority of whom are not white people. And they measure him by the way he treats the nonwhite people here in America. This integration talk is hypocrisy, meant to impress our brothers in Africa or Asia.

Rustin: Then what you are saying is that you are opposed to integration because it is not meaningful and can't work. If you believe that integration is not possible, then the logic of your position should be that you are seeking to find a piece of territory and go to it. Either you are advocating the continuation of slavery, since you feel we cannot get integration by the methods that I advocate—which is to say the slow, grinding process of integration—or you are proposing separation.

Malcolm X: We believe integration is hypocrisy. If the government has to pass laws to let us into their education system, if they have to pass laws to get the white man to accept us in better housing in their neighborhoods, that is the equivalent of holding a gun to their head, and that is hypocrisy. If the white man were to accept us, without laws being passed, then we would go for it.

Rustin: Do you think that is going to happen?

Malcolm X: Well, your common sense tells you, sir, that it's not going to happen.

Rustin: But if you cannot do it through the constitutional method, and you cannot do it through brotherhood, then what do you see as the future of black people here and why should they stay?

Malcolm X: As any intelligent person can see, the white man is not going to share his wealth with his ex-slaves. But God has taught us that the only solution for the ex-slave and the slave master is separation.

Rustin: Then you do believe in separation.

Malcolm X: We absolutely do believe in separation.

Rustin: Well, are you being logical by saying, "Let's take over a territory, a part of the U.S." or are you saying, "Let's go outside"?

Malcolm X: I think both are logical. The land could be anywhere. When the Honorable Elijah Muhammad teaches us that we have to have some land of our own, it means just that, that we have to have some land of our own. Now if the master's intention is good, since we have been faithful workers, I should say faithful servants, all these years, then it seems he should give us some of these states. . . .

What Do You Believe In?

Rustin: Well, I am a great advocate of nonviolence, but I think all this talk about whether to integrate or not, and getting involved in the economic life of this country might be more interesting to me if I knew where you wanted to lead people. But I don't know where you want to go. And I don't think you do, either.

Malcolm X: Yes we do. We can take some land right here, sir.

Rustin: Yes, but if you do not believe in integration, and they don't love you, do you think they are going to give you ten or twelve states?

Malcolm X: Ah, Mr. Rustin: the predicament that a man is in is what makes him reach certain decisions. America is in the worst predicament of any country in the history of the world.

Rustin: I agree. . . .

Malcolm X: Now what is causing this predicament? The race problem. America's number one problem is the so-called Negro. What must we do? What must I do about this Negro problem? And whenever America is attacked on the race problem, what can she say?

Rustin: She can say a lot.

Malcolm X: What?

Rustin: I'll tell you what. I have spent twenty-five years of my life on the race question, and I have been twenty-two times to jail. America can say that until 1954, Negroes could not go to school with whites. Now they can. Negroes could not join trade unions, but now they can. I do not say any of this is perfect, but it is enough for America to be able to answer Russia and China and the rest on the race question and, more important, it is enough to keep the great majority of Negroes feeling that things can improve here. Until you have some place to go to, they are going to want to stay here.

Now, I want to stop right here and get something clear. In [Elijah] Muhammad's mind, this may be a religious matter, but in the minds of his followers the Muslim movement is a psychological and political concept. They do not read the Koran, they read the Bible. They are essentially, culturally, Christian, not Muslims. Why therefore do they call themselves Muslims? Because they do not want to use the same religious terminology that their masters used.

Most Negroes who were brought to America came from the West coast of Africa, long before the spread of Islam to that part of Africa. . . .

Malcolm X: That is what the white man taught you . . . after stripping you of your original culture. Now consider the Mali empire—this shows the influence of the Muslim religion in West Africa before the discovery of America.

Rustin: I am not putting down the culture of West Africa, I am just saying that the Islamic influence came later. All over West Africa you will find wonderful sculptures which were the sources for much twentieth century European art, notably Picasso and Cubism. Now these figures could not have been made if the influence of Islam had prevailed, because, as you ought to know, Muslims are not allowed to create figures in their art objects.

Malcolm X: Let me quote from the *Times* last Sunday. It says that Islam is spreading like wildfire in Nigeria and Christianity is only skin-deep.

Who Are the Exploiters?

Host: Does progress involve a greater sense of racial identity?

Rustin: I believe it is very important to have a great sense of racial identity because I believe it is quite impossible for people to struggle creatively if they do not truly believe in themselves. I believe that dignity is first. This for me is doubly important because believing in integration and not being told where we are to go, I can see nothing more logical than staying here and struggling for one's rights. Also because of moral principles—but leave them aside for the moment—I can see no way for the Negro to struggle except through non-violence and a dedication to a strategic non-violence as a matter of principle. Now therefore if you are going to struggle with non-violence to a certain extent you are going to have a certain affection for the people who are mistreating you. Now affection for the other fellow is not possible without a great sense of dignity of oneself and therefore the dignity of the Negro for me is not something that is an aside. It is an essential of the struggle. The people in Montgomery [Alabama] were able to struggle and get integration on their buses for a simple reason: ten years before they could not have done it because they did not believe in themselves. When they believed in themselves they could be socially affectionate to the opposition while at the same time they could be extremely militant and walking and being prepared to sacrifice. I think this is most important and I would therefore agree with Malcolm X that doing away with the ugliness resulting from poverty and their position in society is very necessary and important. We can certainly agree here.

But now let me ask you another question because I want to clarify your position on the Jewish question. Where do you and your group come out on this question? I've been given to understand that your position is—particularly in Harlem—that one of the reasons that Negroes are so oppressed is that the Jews are exploiting them and that the Jews are attempting to exploit the Arab world and stir up difficulties in the Middle East. I'd like to know if this is a misunderstanding I have.

Malcolm X: If you have read what the Honorable Elijah Muhammad has written and he has written much, I don't think you can find an article where he has ever pointed out the Jew as an exploiter of the black man. He speaks of the exploiter. Period. . . . He doesn't break it down in terms of Frenchmen or an Englishman or a Jew or a German, He speaks of the exploiter and sometimes the man who is the most guilty of exploitation will think you are pointing the finger at him and put out the propaganda that you're anti-this or anti-that. We make no distinction between exploitation and exploiter.

Rustin: Now what do you mean that the man who is the most exploited will put out propaganda?

Malcolm X: I say this that when a man puts out propaganda against Muslims usually that man feels that the finger is being pointed at him but. . . .

Rustin: In other words, you feel that many Jews feel that way.

Malcolm X: I don't know. But I say that you cannot find anything that the Honorable Elijah Muhammad has written or said that at anytime will label the Jew as an exploiter. No sir, but he speaks about the exploitation and oppression and the deception that has been used against the black people in America. Now the man that is guilty (let) whoever is guilty wear that shoe. But he has never made that distinction between a Frenchman—and again—or a Jew or a German. An exploiter is an exploiter, I don't care what kind of label you put on him—you can't duck it.

Kennedy Wins the Presidency by a Slim Margin

By Theodore C. Sorensen

Author Theodore C. Sorensen analyzes several factors that earned John F. Kennedy the presidency in November 1960. He believes the television debate against Republican candidate Vice President Richard Nixon was pivotal. Because Kennedy appeared youthful and energetic while Nixon looked tired and scruffy, the debates helped Kennedy win over many television viewers. Kennedy's intensive campaign also worked for him, demonstrating his convictions and quick wit in public forums. And Kennedy enjoyed a huge vote from blacks in the South because of his compassion for the work of Martin Luther King Jr. Sorensen also attributes part of Kennedy's victory to Lyndon B. Johnson, Kennedy's running mate, who campaigned vigorously and earned the loyalty of southern states. Despite this support, Kennedy won the 1960 election against Richard Nixon by a very slim margin.

Theodore C. Sorensen served as a special assistant and counsel to President Kennedy. He is the author of *Decision-Making in the White House, The Kennedy Legacy, "Let the Word Go Forth": The Speeches, Statements, and Writings of John F. Kennedy*, and *Kennedy*, a 1965 biography from which this article was taken.

The minute [John F. Kennedy] awoke around nine the next morning, I mounted the stairs and congratulated him on his election as President. "What happened in California?" were his first words. I told him—mistakenly as it turned out—that he had carried California and that, in any event, he had carried Minnesota, Michigan and Illinois as well as Pennsylvania and Missouri, to guarantee an electoral majority. . . .

His popular vote margin continued to dwindle, dropping finally to less than 120,000 out of nearly 69 million votes cast (in contrast with his electoral vote margin of 303-219). When the gracious wires of concession and congratulation finally came shortly after noon from Nixon and [retiring president Dwight D.] Eisenhower (after the Minnesota verdict was final), he was all business, deliberating his replies and his statement of victory. His elation over achieving the long-sought prize of the Presidency was tempered by the fatigue that had finally caught up with him, by the responsibilities that lay ahead of him and by the narrowness of his hard-won victory.

What accounted for Kennedy's victory after his initial lag in the polls? The margin was so narrow that almost any important aspect of the campaign could probably be said to have provided the final margin. In my view, any list of decisive factors in Kennedy's favor, excluding his defensive actions on religion, would have to include the following seven, without attempting to ascribe relative weight to any one of them:

The Television Debates

Kennedy's sincerity and vitality, in the most televised campaign in history, and in the televised debates in particular, appealed to millions of voters who would otherwise have dismissed him as too young or known nothing about him but his religion. One survey showed four million voters making up their minds on the basis of the debates, with a three-to-one margin for Kennedy.

Nixon, confident of his superior debating experience, did not avail himself of the many excuses he could have employed to refuse Kennedy's challenge to debate, and thereby gave the far lesser-known Senator his most highly publicized forum and most highly prized opportunity of the entire election campaign. Handicapped in the vital first debate by a poor television appearance, and hoping to win Democratic votes by erasing the image of the "old" more militant Nixon, he enabled Kennedy to appear more vigorous by seemingly agreeing with many of the Senator's most pointed thrusts.

Kennedy's campaign style, tested and sharpened in seven spring primaries, was more attractive, more vigorous and more consistently on the offensive. Driving hard from the outset, he appealed to an inner feeling that the soft and easy life was not enough, that our national potential was unfulfilled. . . . Subsequent analysis by the University of Michigan showed that, contrary to our fears of a late Nixon "tide," Kennedy won two to one among those making up their minds in the last two weeks before election. Indeed, had more time permitted, he might have carried such additional states as Virginia, Florida and California. His incredibly intensive campaign had convinced the unconvinced, projected his own convictions, demonstrated his quick intelligence, converted his youth into an asset and showed Democratic anti-Catholics that he was not only a Catholic.

Nixon's campaign effort, handicapped at the outset by two weeks in the hospital with an infected knee, and further diluted by the fulfillment of his convention pledge to speak in all fifty states, had less substance and style than Kennedy's. In contrast to the Kennedy theory on timing, Nixon's strategy called for a careful pacing of campaign efforts, going all out the last two weeks to reach his peak on Election Eve, but his pacing was too slow and his peak fell short.

Party Identification

Kennedy's party, despite Eisenhower's personal appeal and successive victories, was the majority party in this country in terms of both registration and voting below the Presidential level. The majority of Senators, Congressmen, governors and big-city mayors were Democrats, capable of helping with organization and registration; and Kennedy appealed strongly and frequently to party unity, history and loyalty. To make the most of this majority, a highly skilled well-organized registration drive helped bring out nearly seven million more people than voted four years earlier, over four million of whom it was assumed were Democrats.

Nixon wished to be identified in the campaign with Eisenhower, but not with his party, not with all his policies and not at the expense of his own independence. At the outset, neither Nixon nor Eisenhower seemed certain of their relation or the extent to which the President's participation in the campaign might overshadow the Vice President. Kennedy meanwhile was placing Nixon on the defensive for all the failings of the preceding years. The full-scale entry of Eisenhower, whose immense popularity more than made up for his lack of political enthusiasm, was thus delayed until it was too late to switch enough states.

Running Mate

Kennedy's running mate, Lyndon Johnson, helped salvage several Southern states the Republicans had counted on capturing, with an intensive campaign mixture of carrots and sticks, and campaigned effectively in some forty states. The maltreatment to which he and his wife were subjected by a shoving, booing crowd of disorderly Republican fanatics in Dallas undoubtedly helped switch more than the 23,000 voters who provided the Democratic margin in Texas; and had it not been for the return of Texas and Louisiana to the Democratic column from their 1956 Republican sojourn, and for the Carolinas' staying Democratic against a predicted Republican victory, Nixon would have won the election.

Nixon's running mate, Henry Cabot Lodge—whom the press and pollsters (but never Senator Kennedy) all said would strengthen the Republican ticket more than Johnson would help the Democrats—proved to be the least industrious campaigner on either ticket; and both his blatant pledge of a Negro in the Nixon Cabinet and his subsequent vacillation on the matter offended voters of all areas and races. Lodge was nationally known as "the man from the UN"; and had more political appeal than either Secretary of Labor James Mitchell, whom Nixon might have selected in pursuit of Catholic votes had Kennedy not been nominated, or Senator Thruston Morton of Kentucky, whom Nixon might have selected in pursuit of Southern votes had Johnson not been nominated. . . .

Negro-Southern Choices

Kennedy's phone call of concern and interest to the bereaved and pregnant wife of Negro leader Martin Luther King, imprisoned in Georgia on a traffic technicality—a call which almost all his advisers initially opposed as a futile "grandstand" gesture which would cost more votes among Southerners than it would gain among Negroes—was hailed throughout the Negro community, which then voted overwhelmingly for Kennedy in numbers exceeding his margin of victory in several Northern and Southern states. . . .

Nixon's hope of an unprecedented Republican Southern sweep kept him quiet on the Rev. King's fate, and also caused him during the final week to neglect close states in the North for a flying and futile trip to South Carolina and Texas.

Foreign Policy

By chance, an American U-2 "spy" plane had been downed in Russia in the spring of 1960. The subsequent break-up of the Paris Summit Conference, cancellation of Eisenhower's trips to the Soviet Union and Japan, public fear of a space and missile lag and the increasing realization that the Communists controlled Cuba "only ninety miles from our shore," all clouded the atmosphere of "peace" which a year earlier had seemed certain to silence any Democratic critic. Nixon, dependent on Eisenhower's goodwill, and defensive of the Republican record, was required to make rosy assertions about American leadership and prestige abroad which Kennedy continually exploded.

Recession

In the last month of the campaign, the nation could clearly feel the effects of a recession which had actually started in April, three months after Eisenhower predicted "the most prosperous year in our history." It was the third recession in seven years, giving urban voters in the large industrial states good reason to be dissatisfied. Kennedy, on the offensive, was able to emphasize the downturn; Nixon publicly denied its existence and privately failed to persuade his administration to take sufficient action to counteract it. The Federal Reserve Board, as he urged, loosened credit in June but this was not enough. The votes of newly unemployed workers alone in Illinois, New Jersey, Michigan, Minnesota, Missouri and South Carolina were greater than Kennedy's margin in those states, and their electoral votes were greater than his margin in the Electoral College. Nixon ran worst not, as many believe, in the cities with the highest proportion of Catholics but in the cities with the highest proportion of unemployed.

Catholicism Worked Against Him

Each of these seven factors worked in Kennedy's favor. This was fortunate, for the eighth and by far the largest factor in the campaign worked against him: religion. Obviously there were other reasons for Protestants and others to vote against him—or for him. I cannot agree with Ambassador Joseph Kennedy, who, when asked how many states his son would have carried had he been an Episcopalian, snapped without hesitation: "Fifty!" Most of the more superficial analyses completed immediately after the election concluded that Kennedy's religion had on balance helped him. But subsequent studies in depth concluded that it was, other than Republican Party loyalty, the strongest factor against him.

Catholic voters were not uniformly Kennedy's strongest supporters. Conservative, well-to-do and suburban Catholics con-

John F. Kennedy's ease in front of the camera and quick wit in public forums helped him win over voters.

tinued to vote Republican, particularly in the West, Midwest and upper New England. Among the states listed in the Bailey Memorandum, Catholic votes for Nixon helped the Republican ticket carry Ohio, Wisconsin, New Hampshire, Montana and California.

Nevertheless Kennedy's religion was undoubtedly a help in bringing back to the national Democratic ticket most of the Catholic Democrats who had twice preferred Eisenhower to [Adlai] Stevenson while still considering themselves Democrats and voting Democratic locally. More than three out of five Catholics who voted for Eisenhower in 1956 switched to Kennedy in 1960. Hardly any of them, however, were regular Republicans. Most analysts agree that their return to the Democratic column in 1960 was likely anyway for any candidate, Protestant or Catholic, with the probable exception of Stevenson. But to what extent these Catholic Democrats were *also* moved by pride in Kennedy's religion, by resentment of the attacks upon it, or foreign policy, economics or a dozen other reasons, cannot ever be measured. . . .

What is certain is that had Kennedy not scored large majorities among other types of voters, including Negroes, Jews and union members—had he not convinced almost as many Protestants as Catholics who had voted for Eisenhower to switch to him—he would not have won the election. His increased support from Catholics alone would not have been sufficient to secure him a plurality in Connecticut, Delaware, Illinois, Maryland, New Jersey, New York, Nevada or any of the Southern and border states he recaptured. In Massachusetts, Rhode Island, Michigan, Pennsylvania and possibly Minnesota, the return of Catholic voters to the Democratic ticket may well have been one of the keys to the electoral votes of those five states returning to the Democratic column, but these electoral gains alone clearly would not have been enough to beat Nixon. . . .

Kennedy's over-all loss nationally from Protestant Democrats, reported the University of Michigan survey, was at least 4.5 million votes, far more than any Catholic vote gains could offset. In terms of electoral votes, the five states in which the return of Catholic votes helped supply his winning margin outweighed those states which can be clearly identified as lost because of religion. But the Michigan survey analysts, convinced that most of the Catholics voting for Kennedy would have returned to the Democratic fold anyway, concluded that Kennedy's religion prevented him from winning by a comfortable popular majority. And Professor V.O. Key, Jr. summed up the results of the later surveys with the judgment "that Kennedy won in spite of rather than because of the fact that he was a Catholic."

The Mandate of the People

The fact remains that he won, and on the day after election, and every day thereafter, he rejected the argument that the country had given him no mandate. Every election has a winner and a loser, he said in effect. "The margin is narrow, but the responsibility is clear. There may be difficulties with the Congress, but a margin of only one vote would still be a mandate.". . .

As he watched the election returns on the night of November 8, and reviewed them in the weeks that followed, he had reason for both satisfaction and disappointment. He had never counted on any support from the rural, Protestant, conservative states of the Midwest and West. Farm labor supported him more strongly than farm owners. . . . He had been hopeful but had not counted on winning Nevada and New Mexico (nor had he counted on Delaware in the East. He won all three). He knew Utah and Idaho were no contest once the head of the Mormon Church (long wooed by Kennedy) endorsed Nixon, even though Kennedy ran well ahead of the 1956 Democratic vote in every county in both states. But he was as surprised at his loss of Alaska as he was by his win in Hawaii (where it was not clear that he had won until a December 28 recount).

He had held some hopes for Montana, and possibly even Colorado, where the Denver *Post* had given him its first Democratic Presidential endorsement since 1916. He lost both. He was disappointed that National Chairman [Henry] Jackson had not been able to deliver Washington. He was chagrined at not having spent more time in California, where migrants from the Bible Belt to the central valley had switched to Nixon in sufficient numbers to defeat him in a contest so close it was decided by the Republican absentee voters. That is why, conceding the strongly anti-Catholic Oklahoma, he had sent its Governor to campaign for him in the rural centers of California—but to no avail. Democratic factionalism had undermined him there as well.

The other state where a lack of time and unity defeated him was Virginia. "We could take this state away from Harry Byrd if we only had more time," he had said to me leaving Roanoke less than a week earlier, but we did not have time and fell short by

42,000 votes out of more than three-quarter million cast.

He had counted on most of the larger, more urbanized and in-dustrial states of the Midwest, but expected to lose (and did lose) Indiana, where his reception seemed the coolest of the entire cam-paign. He won in Minnesota, with the help of Hubert Humphrey, where his victory was due more to the depressed Mesabi Iron Range than to the big cities. ("I used to think the Democrats were pretty strong in South Boston," he had said in Hibbing, "but we are going to send them out here for indoctrination.") He won in Illinois, where he was helped by strong candidates for Governor and Senator, Otto Kerner and his old friend Senator [Paul] Doug-las. He barely won in Missouri and in Michigan. He lost Wis-consin, where he had hoped his spring primary efforts would overcome a built-in Republican edge.

But his biggest disappointment by far was Ohio, where his Harris Poll had showed him ahead. In few states had he spent so much time or had larger or more enthusiastic crowds. Although he increased the Democratic vote in Ohio over 1956 by the same proportion as he did elsewhere, and increased it in 96 percent of its counties, that was not enough. . . .

With these exceptions—and the exceptions of Ohio, Califor-nia, Wisconsin and Virginia made all the difference between a massive victory and a narrow squeak—the electoral results were about as he had hoped and expected. (My own expectations, as recorded in an office pool, had been too optimistic. I had pre-dicted 408 electoral votes, lower than some of my colleagues but far above his final total of 303, to which Pierre Salinger came closest in our group. All of us predicted his proportion of the two-party popular vote would be in the 53–57 percent range, not in the 50.1–50.2 percent range it ultimately was.)

The Narrowest of Victories

Candidate Kennedy had known that he had a tough fight, taking on a powerfully entrenched administration that had brought on no war or depression. He had known, reviewing Eisenhower's margins in 1956, that it would be no easy task to change enough voters to regain enough states. Both his own polls and the pub-lished ones told him it would be close nationally and close in the key states, but he could not have known it would be the closest in seventy-six years. He won twelve states with less than 2 per-cent of the two-party vote and lost six in the same range.

He had known also that no significant number of Republicans—Catholics or any other kind—would shift to him (and they didn't), and that to offset the loss of Democratic Protestants he had to pick up even more members of all faiths who had voted for Eisenhower (and he did). He had known that he would have to convert the sizable Republican majorities of 1956 in the major industrial states—an Eisenhower plurality of more than a million and a half in New York alone, for example—into new Democratic majorities (and he did).

He had known he would have to win a tremendous vote from labor, Catholics, Negroes, Jews, young voters and other city dwellers, and break even in the suburbs if he was to offset the rural and small-town Republican vote. He did. He broke even in the total vote cast in thirty-seven major suburban areas, carried twelve of the nineteen most important and increased the Democratic vote in all but one. He carried twenty-six of the forty largest cities, compared to Stevenson's four years earlier carrying only eleven. Of the fourteen Nixon carried all were in the Midwest, West or South (the one big city most opposed to Kennedy was Dallas, Texas).

Finally, he had gambled that Lyndon Johnson would not hurt him in the North and would help him in the South. That gamble paid off. Nixon, who emphasized states' rights in the South, had consistently criticized Johnson's nomination in the North—but with no effect. The Liberal Party in New York, which had threatened at Los Angeles to nominate its own ticket because of Johnson, cast more votes for Kennedy and Johnson than the margin by which they carried the state. In the South, where Johnson had wisely spent nearly half the campaign, the Democratic ticket, despite a growing tide of Republicanism, racism and religious bigotry, regained from the Republican column not only Texas—with the help of a large Negro and Latin-American vote, and resentment of the Johnsons' mistreatment in Dallas—but also Louisiana, where an independent elector movement split the opposition. . . .

The Michigan survey estimated that the religious issue alone cost Kennedy an estimated net loss of one out of every six Southern voters, more than enough to account for Nixon's margin in Florida, Kentucky, and Virginia, as well as Tennessee, Oklahoma and possibly other Southern, border and Western states. . . .

But the very narrowness of his victory had, in another sense, broadened its base. John Kennedy could not have been elected

President without the votes he received from Protestants as well as Catholics and Jews—indeed, more Protestants voted for him than all his Catholic and Jewish supporters combined. He could not have been elected without both Negro and Southern support. He could not have won without the votes he received from farmers and businessmen, young and old, rich and poor, cities and suburbs. His victory actually related to regions, religions and races only in the minds of the analysts. Millions of Americans who fitted into no category other than "citizens," and who acted on the basis of no pressure other than their own convictions, elected John Kennedy President of the United States.

One week earlier he had assailed an anonymous Republican poster distributed to San Diego defense plant workers which bore the caption: "Jack Kennedy is after your job." "That shows," he said, "how desperate and despicable this campaign has become. . . . I am after Mr. Eisenhower's job."

Now—after an uphill fight, against all odds, breaking all precedents and by the narrowest of margins—the job was his. That he had won at all, he admitted upon reflection, was "a miracle."

CHRONOLOGY

January 1: Soviet premier Nikita Khrushchev indicates in a New Year's toast that the Soviet Union might disarm unilaterally if it fails to reach an arms agreement with the West.

January 4: The longest steel strike in the nation's history ends as steel companies and the United Steel Workers agree on a wage increase. The strike had started in July 1959.

January 9: The Protestant Episcopal Church approves the use of artificial birth control.

February 1: Four black students start a sit-in protest against segregation at a Woolworth department store in Greensboro, North Carolina; the protest inspires more sit-ins and demonstrations throughout the South in the following months; lunch counters in Greensboro finally desegregate in July.

February 8: France detonates an atomic bomb in the Sahara, becoming the world's fourth nuclear power after the United States, the Soviet Union, and Great Britain.

February 16: Black protests against segregation in public facilities spread to five states.

February 18: The Winter Olympics begins in Squaw Valley, California.

February 27–29: Black students protest segregated stores in Nashville, Tennessee, leading to some arrests; Nashville department stores begin desegregating in May.

February 28: Klansmen meet in Atlanta to form the Knights of the Ku Klux Klan, a group violently opposed to the integration of blacks in American society.

February 29: The U.S. Supreme Court upholds voting rights of blacks.

March: The student boycott of commercial establishments in the South gains support from more established civil rights groups like the Southern Christian Leadership Conference (SCLC), National Association for the Advancement of Colored People (NAACP), and Congress of Racial Equality (CORE); students in schools such as Harvard, Yale, Princeton, University of Chicago, and University of California at Berkeley start supporting southern students.

March 26: The U.S. Court of Appeals lifts the ban on D.H. Lawrence's *Lady Chatterley's Lover*, ruling that the novel is a great work of art and can be shipped to readers through the mail.

April 1: The United States launches *Tiros 1* (Television and Infrared Observation Satellite), the first satellite that provides a worldwide weather observation system.

April 15–17: Black students organize the Student Nonviolent Coordinating Committee (SNCC) at Shaw University in Raleigh, North Carolina, to serve as a coordinating body for students and young people; the organization vows to use only nonviolent means to press for integration and other reforms.

April 28: The general assembly of the Presbyterian Church (Southern) declares that marital sexual relations without the intent of procreation are not sinful.

May 1: A U.S. U-2 spy plane flies into Soviet space and is shot down by the Soviet military; Soviet premier Nikita Khrushchev warns that the incident might lead to war; the incident sends jitters all over the world and scuttles the Paris disarmament meeting scheduled later in the year.

May 2: Caryl Chessman is executed after staying on San Quentin's death row in California for twelve years; the execution sparks local and global protests.

May 6: President Eisenhower signs the 1960 Civil Rights Act, making it law; it reaffirms the voting rights for all Americans, protects the right of black Americans to vote, and penalizes obstructions to voter registration.

May 9: A U.S. district court orders Atlanta, Georgia, to begin desegregation of schools in September 1961; the Food and Drug Administration (FDA) approves the sale of oral contraceptives;

Enovid 10, the first oral contraceptive pill, is first sold at fifty-five cents a pill.

May 10: Nashville integrates six lunch counters in first such action in the South. Massachusetts senator John F. Kennedy, a Roman Catholic, wins the West Virginia primary, proving that he can attract support in a predominantly Protestant state.

May 13: In San Francisco students protest the activities of the House Un-American Activities Committee (HUAC); police use fire hoses to stop the demonstrators; scores are arrested; the incident signals the beginning of student radical action.

May 27: The United States ends aid to Cuba after Fidel Castro appoints Communists to his cabinet and his ties with the Soviet Union become clear.

May 31: The President's Joint Commission on Mental Illness and Health reports 25 percent of Americans suffer from mental illness at some point in their lives.

June 23: In Arlington, Virginia, Hot Shoppes becomes the first national chain to desegregate.

July 13: Massachusetts senator John F. Kennedy wins the Democratic presidential nomination; Lyndon B. Johnson is nominated for vice president.

July 25: Vice President Richard M. Nixon wins the Republican presidential nomination.

July 27: At the Geneva nuclear test-ban talks the United States, Great Britain, and the Soviet Union agree to bar atmospheric tests as well as underground detonations registering more than 4.75 on the Richter scale.

July 31: Elijah Muhammad, spiritual head of the Nation of Islam, calls for the creation of a separate state for blacks.

August 16: A total of sixty-nine southern towns integrate.

August 27: Race riots erupt in Jacksonville, Florida, after ten days of sit-ins.

September 26: Kennedy and Nixon meet in the first televised debate between presidential candidates; the debate, in four segments, is watched by 75 million Americans.

October 17: Four national chain stores report that lunch counters in 112 towns have been integrated.

October 22: After a demonstration, Martin Luther King Jr. is arrested in Atlanta for violating an earlier traffic sentence; with the intervention of presidential nominee, Massachusetts senator John F. Kennedy, and his brother Robert Kennedy, King is released on October 26.

November 8: Kennedy defeats Nixon in the U.S. presidential elections by a slender margin of less than 120,000 votes.

November 12: The U.S. Justice Department warns Louisiana governor Jimmie Davis against blocking desegregation of public schools.

November 13: A special session of the Louisiana legislature approves drastic steps to avoid New Orleans school desegregation.

November 16: In Washington, D.C., President Eisenhower orders restraints on overseas spending to stop the outflow of gold from the United States; in New Orleans, hundreds of residents riot in the streets against integration.

November 17: The Central Intelligence Agency briefs president-elect Kennedy on plans to invade Cuba.

December 4: New Orleans black minister Floyd Foreman continues to escort his five-year-old daughter to an integrated neighborhood school despite abuse.

December 5: The U.S. Supreme Court rules that racial discrimination in restaurants at bus terminals serving interstate bus passengers violates the Interstate Commerce Act.

FOR FURTHER RESEARCH

Art and Culture

Lawrence Alloway, *American Pop Art.* New York: Macmillan, 1974.

Bruce Cook, *The Beat Generation.* New York: Charles Scribner's Sons, 1971.

Ellen H. Johnson, ed., *American Artists on Art: From 1940 to 1980.* New York: Harper & Row, 1982.

Jane Stern and Michael Stern, *Sixties People.* New York: Alfred A. Knopf, 1990.

The Cold War

Michael R. Beschloss, *May-Day: Eisenhower, Khrushchev, and the U-2 Affair.* New York: Harper & Row, 1986.

Laurence Chang and Peter Kornbluh, eds., *The Cuban Missile Crisis, 1962: A National Security Archive Documents Reader.* New York: New Press, 1998.

Richard Ned Lebow and Janice Gross Stein, *We All Lost the Cold War.* Princeton, NJ: Princeton University Press, 1994.

Francis Gary Powers with Curt Gentry, *Operation Overflight: The U-2 Spy Pilot Tells His Story for the First Time.* New York: Holt, Rinehart and Winston, 1970.

Wayne S. Smith, *The Closest of Enemies.* New York: W.W. Norton, 1987.

David Wise and Thomas Ross, *The U-2 Affair.* New York: Random House, 1962.

The Presidency

Stephen E. Ambrose, *Eisenhower.* New York: Simon and Schuster, 1984.

Elmo Richardson, *The Presidency of Dwight D. Eisenhower.* Lawrence: Regents Press of Kansas, 1979.

Theodore C. Sorensen, *Kennedy.* New York: Harper & Row, 1965.

Society and Politics

Jules Archer, *The Incredible Sixties.* San Diego: Harcourt Brace Jovanovich, 1986.

Ronald Berman, *America in the Sixties: An Intellectual History.* New York: Free Press, 1968.

Hugh Davis Graham and Ted Robert Gurr, eds., *Violence in America: Historical and Comparative Perspectives.* New York: New American Library, 1969.

Theodore Hamm, *Rebel and a Cause: Caryl Chessman and the Politics of the Death Penalty in Postwar California, 1948– 1974.* Los Angeles: University of California Press, 2001.

James Haskins and Kathleen Benson, eds., *The 1960s Reader.* New York: Viking Kestrel, 1988.

Lauren Kessler, *After All These Years: Sixties Ideas in a Different World.* New York: Thunder's Mouth, 1990.

Arthur Marwick, *The Sixties: Cultural Revolution in Britain, France, Italy, and the United States.* Oxford: Oxford University Press, 1998.

Loretta McLaughlin, *The Pill, John Rock, and the Church: The Biography of a Revolution.* Boston: Little, Brown, 1982.

Theodore Roszak, *The Making of a Counter Culture.* Garden City, NY: Doubleday, 1972.

Massimo Teodori, ed., *The New Left: A Documentary History.* Indianapolis: Bobbs-Merrill, 1969.

Irwin Unger and Debi Unger, eds., *The Times Were a Changin':The Sixties Reader.* New York: Three Rivers, 1998.

Milton Viorst, *Fire in the Streets: America in the 1960s.* New York: Simon and Schuster, 1979.

Student Protests and the Civil Rights Movement

Terry H. Anderson, *The Movement and the Sixties: Protest in America from Greensboro to Wounded Knee.* New York: Oxford University Press, 1995.

Taylor Branch, *America in the King Years: 1954–1963.* New York: Simon and Schuster, 1988.

Clayborne Carson, *In Struggle: SNCC and the Black Awakening of the 1960s.* Cambridge: Harvard University Press, 1981.

Clayborne Carson et al., eds., *Eyes on the Prize: Civil Rights Reader.* New York: Penguin, 1991.

Marshall Frady, *Martin Luther King, Jr.* New York: Viking, 1992.

Mary King, *Freedom Song.* New York: William Morrow, 1987.

Alan F. Westin, ed., *Freedom Now! The Civil Rights Struggle in America.* New York: BasicBooks, 1964.

Sanford Wexler, *The Civil Rights Movement: An Eyewitness History.* New York: Facts On File, 1993.

Summing Up the Decade

John Brooks, *The Great Leap: The Past Twenty-Five Years in America.* New York: Harper & Row, 1966.

David Farber, ed., *The Sixties: From Memory to History.* Chapel Hill: University of North Carolina Press, 1994.

Richard Layman, *The American Decades: 1960–1969.* Detroit, MI: Gale Research, 1995

Anthony Lewis, *Portrait of a Decade.* New York: Random House, 1964.

Myron Magnet, *The Dream and the Nightmare: The Sixties' Legacy to the Underclass.* New York: William Morrow, 1993.

William L. O'Neill, *Coming Apart: An Informal History of America in the 1960s.* Chicago: Quadrangle, 1971.

Barbara L. Tischler, ed., *Sights on the Sixties.* New Brunswick, NJ: Rutgers University Press, 1992.

Neville Williams, ed., *Chronology of World History.* Vol. 4. Santa Barbara, CA: ABC-CLIO, 1999.

Websites

The Civil Rights Movement in America, www.historylearningsite. co.uk. The website offers information on various periods of world history, including U.S. history. The civil rights section focuses on leaders, organizations, highlights, time lines, and other aspects of the movement.

Digital History: Using Technologies to Enhance Teaching and Research, www.digitalhistory.uh.edu. Digital History has resource guides, an encyclopedia, biographies, essays, primary sources, and government records on various historical periods, including the sixties.

Greensboro Sit-ins: Launch of a Civil Rights Movement, www. sitins.com. The website has information on the sit-ins in the South that began with a small protest in Greensboro, North Carolina, including interviews with participants, a time line of the civil rights movement, photos, audio materials, and links to related sites.

1960 Civil Rights Timeline, www.geocities.com. The website presents a comprehensive time line of the civil rights movement in 1960.

The Sixties Project, www.lists.village.virginia.edu. The Sixties Project has documents on the student movement and the anti-war movement.

INDEX

see also Student Nonviolent
  Coordinating Committee
Students for a Democratic Society
  (SDS), 85
Summer Place, A (film), 35
Supreme Court, U.S., 15, 38
Syntex Laboratories, 51

Tabloid Publishing Company, 43
teen pregnancy, 54–55
television
  civil rights movement and, 16, 20,
    26
  election of 1960 and, 103–104
  films and, 36
Tennessee, 86, 92
Teodori, Massimo, 56
Time (magazine), 49, 94
Tisdale, Geneva, 24–25, 26, 27

University of California at Berkeley,
  17, 57–59
Urban League, 14
U.S. News & World Report
  (magazine), 94
U-2. *See* planes, spy

Valiant, 29, 30–31
Vietnam, 12
Volkswagen, 32
Volvo, 32
voter registration drives, 89, 92

Ward's Automotive Report, 30
Woolworth stores, 13–14, 19–21,
  23, 27
Wright, James, 29, 31, 32

Zane, Ed, 27
Zinsser, William K., 34

973.921   1960.
196

DATE			